BEGINNER'S GUIDE TO SELLING YOUR CRAFTS ON ETSY

BY ANN ECKHART

Table of Contents

INTRODUCTION

Crafting is a passion for millions of people around the world. From knitting and woodworking to pottery and jewelry-making, people love creating unique and beautiful items with their own hands. And while many crafters sell their products at local vendor fairs and markets, a whole world of potential customers is waiting online. Customers who have a lot of disposable income or who can't easily get out to local sales shop extensively online, including on crafted items. Yet many crafters fear making the jump to online sales, fearing it is too complicated or just trying to figure out where to start.

That's where Etsy comes in. You've likely already heard of Etsy, the online marketplace where millions of buyers find handmade and vintage items from around the world. Makers around the globe sell their wares on Etsy to supplement their local sales. And some sell exclusively on Etsy, earning a full-time income that far surpasses what they could make if they only sold locally. Etsy sellers have the potential to reach a massive audience and grow their businesses beyond their wildest dreams.

And you can, too!

Etsy refers to its craft sellers as "makers." While you can also sell antiques, print-on-demand products, and digital items on the site, when most people think of Etsy, they think of crafts. Sellers who hand-make jewelry, toys, home décor, personalized clothing, gift baskets, stationery, candles, and more can sell their wares 24/7 to customers across the globe. The best part is that Etsy handles all the hard stuff, such as payment processing, shipping labels, and sales tax collection. As a crafter, you can focus on creating and selling while Etsy handles the rest.

But getting started on Etsy can be intimidating, especially for those with little computer experience or those who have never sold online. Questions such as how to set up an Etsy shop, how to list products, and the biggest one, how to ship orders, keep many potential craft sellers from even trying to branch out to Etsy.

But selling on Etsy isn't hard if you have someone to help you. And that's where this book comes in! I have been selling online since 2005 on sites such as Amazon, eBay, Poshmark, and Etsy; and I know the ins and outs of selling on the Etsy platform. I know all of the tips and tricks, and I know how to explain them in a way that anyone can understand.

In *Beginner's Guide to Selling Your Crafts on Etsy*, I'll walk you through setting up and growing your Etsy shop. I'll cover everything you need to know, including:

- Why Etsy is the best place to sell your crafts
- What crafts sell best on Etsy
- How to set up your Etsy account
- How to open an Etsy shop
- Step-by-step instructions for listing your crafts for sale on Etsy
- Step-by-step instructions for shipping out orders
- How to market and advertise your Etsy shop
- How to handle accounting and bookkeeping
- How to deal with customer service issues
- Growing your business on Etsy and beyond

Whether you're a seasoned crafter looking to take your business to the next level or a complete beginner just starting out selling your wares, this book will provide you with the knowledge and tools you need to succeed on Etsy and beyond. Etsy provides makers a way to increase their income from home, which makes it perfect for those with families to take care of or for those who work outside of the house is difficult. No matter what your station in life is, Etsy can work for you.

With just a computer, an internet connection, a smartphone for taking photos, and some shipping supplies, you can start making money selling your crafts on Etsy. So if you are ready to break free of poorly attended local craft shows and your oversaturated area market, let's get you started selling on Etsy!

CHAPTER ONE: WHY YOU SHOULD SELL YOUR CRAFTS ON ETSY

As a crafter looking to sell your products online, choosing the right platform is crucial for the success of your business. But with so many online stores to choose from, it's hard to zone in on which is the best for your products. In today's digital age, where online shopping is more popular than ever before, having a strong online presence is essential, even if it is just a Facebook business page. After all, can you really trust a business if they aren't even on Facebook?

But not all online marketplaces are created equal, especially when it comes to selling handmade items. Choosing the right platform can make all the difference in reaching your target audience, increasing your sales, and growing your business. Your unique crafts are likely your passion. You've probably spent months or even years developing your products. But even if you have a loyal local following, sales within your city limits can only take you so far. To grow your craft sales, you need to sell your products online.

While there are many online marketplaces available for selling crafts, Etsy is, without a doubt, the go-to platform for makers around the globe. With over 4 million active sellers and 90 million active buyers, Etsy is the largest online marketplace for handmade items. By selling on Etsy, you have access to a massive audience of potential customers from all over the world, making it easier than ever to reach customers beyond your local community.

But why Etsy, specifically? Etsy has a well-established reputation as a marketplace that values quality, creativity, and community. It began as a site solely dedicated to selling handmade products. And while it has opened up to other goods, crafts are still the primary category. Etsy's focus on handmade products that are unique and well-crafted attracts buyers who are willing to pay a premium for one-of-a-kind items, making it the best platform for crafters looking to sell their products at a higher price point. Not only does Etsy provide you with millions of customers looking to purchase crafts, but those customers are also often willing to pay more than shoppers at your local craft shows.

Why will customers pay more? The first is convenience. Not everyone has access to craft fairs. Or if they do, maybe they aren't seeing what they want from local vendors. On Etsy, there are hundreds of thousands of craft shops, giving customers access to a seemingly limitless number of makers that they can shop from at home any time of the day or night.

The second reason customers on Etsy are often willing to pay more is disposable income. On Etsy, you will reach customers all over the world and find many people who simply have more money to spend. While locally you may have a hard time getting people to pay your asking price, on Etsy you will reach people from other areas that have larger budgets. And those shoppers come to Etsy to spend their extra cash, which may go further for them online than if they shopped in their local areas.

But beyond reputation, audience, and reach, Etsy also offers a range of features and tools specifically designed to help crafters succeed. From customizable shop banners to targeted advertising, from customer review management to shipping labels, Etsy's platform provides a wealth of resources to help you grow your business and make the most of your sales. After all, trying to start a website with payment processing, shipping capabilities, and tax collection and remittance is not only extremely difficult but also expensive. Etsy provides sellers with all of these tools at a low cost.

Ultimately, choosing the right platform is about finding the best fit for your business goals and the types of products you sell. And if you are a maker of handmade goods, Etsy should be at the top of your list. In fact, many crafters only sell their products on Etsy, sometimes abandoning local sales altogether.

Some of the benefits Etsy can offer craft sellers are:

Huge Customer Base: As mentioned earlier, Etsy has over 90 million active buyers from around the world, which means that there are millions of potential customers waiting to discover your products. And unlike a craft show where there may be the same number of attendees as sellers, on Etsy shoppers outnumber shops, meaning you have the potential to get your products in front of more customers in one day than you would in a lifetime of selling locally. By listing your products on Etsy, you can tap into a massive market that would be impossible to reach otherwise.

Strong Reputation: Etsy has been around since 2005, and the site continues to grow every year. Its well-established reputation is enhanced by its seller and buyer protection policies.

Payment Options: Etsy accepts all of the major credit cards, including Visa, Mastercard, American Express, and Discover, along with debit cards, PayPal, Apple Pay, and Google Pay. The ability for buyers to choose their preferred payment method is an important factor in shoppers' trust in the site. As a seller, this means that you aren't limited to accepting only cash and checks as you may be at craft fairs. Etsy's payment system handles all financial transactions; you don't have to process payments or remit sales tax.

Low Start-Up Costs: Compared to other business models, starting an Etsy shop is a cost-effective option. There are no fees to open an Etsy account, and the listing and final value fees are competitive with other online platforms. On Etsy, their 20-cent listing fee covers a four-month period, which is significantly less than the approximately 35-cent fee to list an item for one month on a site like eBay. Additionally, Etsy's final value fees are typically lower than other sites, enabling sellers to keep more of their profits.

Flexibility: Another advantage of selling on Etsy is the flexibility it offers. Crafters can work from home or any location with an internet connection on their laptop or by access to the Etsy Seller App via their smartphone. And if you need to be away from your shop for a bit, you can turn Vacation Mode on, which will keep your shop open but hide your products from buyers until you return. This is also a great feature to use in cases of emergency when you simply can't focus on your business.

Ability To Create A Brand: Developing a brand identity is a crucial aspect of running a successful retail business, whether it's online or offline. A brand identity encompasses the overall look and feel of your store, and Etsy's platform is specifically designed to assist sellers in establishing a personalized brand that reflects their products. Etsy offers a variety of tools, from customizable shop banners to product listings, that enable sellers to present their products in the best light possible to stand out from the competition. Much like decorating a booth at a craft show, Etsy equips sellers with all the necessary resources to create a welcoming and attractive virtual storefront that is just as enticing as an in-person shopping experience.

Access To Valuable Resources: In addition to handling payment processing, shipping labels, and sales tax collection, Etsy offers a range of resources and support to help sellers succeed, including a seller handbook, community forums, and customer support. Etsy regularly updates its platform and features based on seller feedback, which means that it is constantly improving and evolving to meet the needs of its users. And best of all, Etsy offers seller protections where they will protect you against lost packages and unreasonable customer demands. Etsy assumes most of the risk, leaving you free to focus on the creative side of your business.

Understanding Etsy's Fees: All online selling platforms charge sellers fees. Amazon, eBay, Poshmark, Facebook Marketplace, and the popular e-commerce tool Shopify are no exceptions. Some platforms, like Amazon and eBay, charge sellers both listing fees and final value fees. Other sites, such as Poshmark and Mercari, only charge sellers when they sell an item.

Etsy charges fees for both listing products and when an item sells. Here's a breakdown of the fees for selling on Etsy:

Listing Fee: Etsy charges a fee of $0.20 to list an item on the platform for a four-month period. This fee is charged per listing, regardless of the number of items you list. If you end the item before the four-month term, you are not refunded any portion of the listing fee. However, being able to list an item on Etsy for one year only will only cost you $.80, which is the lowest listing fee of all of the major platforms.

Transaction Fee: Etsy charges a transaction fee of 5% on the total cost of the item, including shipping and handling fees. This fee covers the cost of payment processing and is automatically deducted from the seller's payment account. Remember that pay of Etsy's payment processing also includes the site collecting sales tax from customers and remitting that tax to the appropriate states on behalf of sellers. That feature alone is one of the most valuable features any online platform can offer.

Payment Processing Fee: Etsy also charges a payment processing fee of 3% + $0.25 on the total cost of the item, including shipping and handling fees. This fee covers the cost of processing the payment through Etsy's payment system and is deducted from the seller's payment account at the time of the transaction. Remember that Etsy accepts every major credit card, debit card, and PayPal. Most online sellers who sell on their own dedicated websites only accept PayPal, which severely limits their ability to accept payments and can turn off some customers. On Etsy, you as a seller never even see the forms of payments your customers use as Etsy handles it all on their end.

Shipping Fees: Shipping is almost always the number one reason people give me when they tell me they are afraid to sell online. We'll go over shipping Etsy orders in detail later on in this book, but for now, you just need to know that you can pay for and print shipping labels directly on Etsy. You do not need to take packages to the Post Office to be weighed and pay for postage there. You can do it all online from home.

When you list a product for sale on Etsy, you enter the shipping weight for that item. When a customer buys that item, Etsy, in conjunction with the United States Postal Service, calculates the shipping based on the package weight and the zip code to which the order is being shipped. You will be given a list of shipping label options to choose from, and when you make your selection, Etsy will automatically deduct the cost of the label from your balance, give you the label to print, and upload the tracking information to both your account and that of your customer. Easy!

It's important to note that Etsy fees may vary depending on your location and the currency used for your sales. This book is written from the perspective of selling in the United States using American currency. Etsy also offers optional services for sellers, such as promoted listings, which may come with additional fees. We'll discuss these additional services later in this book.

Etsy SEO: Throughout this book, we will discuss the important role of optimizing Etsy SEO, or Search Engine Optimization, to drive traffic to your listings and make sales. Etsy relies heavily on its sellers to maximize their listings to ensure they can be found not only on Etsy but also off the site on search engines like Google.

Optimizing your listings for SEO may sound complicated, but it simply means that you need to use relevant keywords and phrases in your listing titles, descriptions, tags, and shop sections. By repeating important keywords and phrases, you are telling Etsy that these are the most important keywords for that product and that they should be using those words to improve your search ranking and increase the chances of your listings being found by buyers who are searching for products like yours. Additionally, optimizing your photos and adding relevant attributes to your listings can also help improve your search visibility on Etsy.

Advertising: While you can pay for additional Etsy advertising, Etsy advertises on its own across various platforms, not just online but also on television and radio, to promote its products and shops. Etsy promotes its products and sellers on its website and mobile app by showcasing new and popular items on the homepage and category pages. Etsy also has a feature called "Editor's Picks" which features products chosen by Etsy editors.

Etsy is also active across all of the major social media platforms. They have a strong social media presence and regularly promote sellers on platforms such as Instagram, Facebook, and Pinterest. They have a dedicated social media team that works with sellers to create content and promote their products on these platforms. And they regularly partner with brands and celebrities to promote the site.

Etsy also works with Google, which is the most widely used search engine in the world, to ensure that its products and sellers appear in Google search results. This means that when buyers search for products on Google, relevant Etsy listings may appear in the search results. And Etsy uses various other online advertising channels, influencers, and bloggers to promote its products and sellers, including display ads, video ads, and retargeting ads.

Help for sellers: Etsy offers a variety of seller tools and resources, including:

Etsy Seller Handbook: The Seller Handbook is a comprehensive yet easy-to-read resource that offers tips, advice, and guidance on all aspects of selling on Etsy, from setting up your shop to managing orders and promoting your products. It includes articles, tutorials, and videos on topics such as photography, pricing, SEO, and marketing.

Etsy Seller App: The Etsy Seller App, which differs from their shopping app, is a mobile app that allows you to manage your shop and keep track of your sales on-the-go. With the app, you can create and edit listings, view your orders and revenue, respond to customer inquiries, and receive real-time notifications about your shop activity. By enabling notifications, you can be alerted to incoming messages as well as orders.

Etsy Analytics: Etsy Analytics is a tool that provides sellers with data and insights about their shop's performance. It allows you to track your views, visits, and sales, as well as understand where your traffic is coming from and what keywords are driving it. You can use this data to optimize your listings and improve your sales.

Etsy Seller Protection: Etsy protects sellers in case of certain order disputes. This protection can help ensure that sellers are not unfairly penalized in cases where they have fulfilled their obligations and shipped their items to the buyer.

For example, if a seller has shipped an item to a buyer, and the tracking information shows that the item was delivered, but the buyer claims that they did not receive the item, the seller may be eligible for Etsy Seller Protection. By shipping orders through Etsy, sellers can easily provide tracking information as evidence that the item was shipped and delivered to the correct address. If the buyer's claim is found to be invalid, Etsy may side with the seller and release the funds from the sale to the seller's account.

It's important to note that not all order disputes are covered under Etsy Seller Protection. For example, disputes related to item quality or condition, or cases where the seller has not fulfilled their obligations, may not be covered. Additionally, sellers must meet certain eligibility criteria to qualify for Seller Protection, such as providing accurate shipping information and responding to buyer inquiries promptly.

The Bottom Line: Etsy is an established e-commerce website with millions of customers and low fees, providing all the tools and resources needed to take your craft business to the next level. The question isn't "Why should you sell on Etsy?" but rather "Why wouldn't you?"

CHAPTER TWO: WHAT CRAFTS SELL BEST ON ETSY

Etsy allows three types of products to be sold on its website: handmade products, vintage items (20 years or older), and craft supplies. According to Etsy's guidelines, a product is considered handmade if the seller personally creates or makes the item by hand or employs studio employees or an assistant who assists in making the item by hand. Etsy requires sellers to disclose the involvement of any production partners in making their handmade items.

Most crafters who sell their wares on Etsy are producing their items by themselves and with supplies they've purchased at craft stores. If you purchased supplies from a craft store to use in making your handmade products, you do not need to disclose this information to buyers as the finished product is still considered handmade according to Etsy's guidelines. This is because the use of pre-made materials or supplies is universally considered a part of the handmade crafting process.

A production partner, on the other hand, is someone who creates or makes a part or all of a product on behalf of the seller. In this case, the seller is required to disclose the involvement of the production partner in the making of the product, as well as the identity and location of the partner, in the listing description in the *Production Partners* field that is included in each Etsy listing.

To clarify this further, let's look at the following two examples:

1. **A crafter who handmakes dolls using only craft store supplies:** Carla is a crafter who specializes in making handmade dolls. She sources all of her supplies from a local craft store and makes each doll entirely by hand. She designs the dolls, cuts the fabric, stitches the seams, and adds the

finishing touches, such as embroidery and buttons. Because Carla makes each doll by hand using only craft store supplies, she is not required to disclose any production partners in her listings, meaning she does not need to name the craft store where she purchases her supplies.

2. **A crafter who uses production partners to make their dolls:** Jared is a crafter who also makes handmade dolls, but he uses production partners to help with the process. He designs the dolls himself but has a team of seamstresses who assist in cutting and stitching the fabric pieces. Jared also works with a local embroidery shop to add custom designs to the dolls. In this case, Jared would be required to disclose the involvement of his production partners in his listings. He would need to include information about the identity and location of the production partners, even the ones he employs, as well as their role in making the dolls.

So, what kinds of crafts sell best on Etsy? The answer is anything handmade! Well, almost anything.

While Etsy allows sellers to list a wide variety of handmade items on their platform, certain items are prohibited and cannot be sold. And you must learn what NOT to sell on Etsy as attempting to do so could, at the very least, get your listing pulled, or at the very worst, get you suspended from the site permanently. And once you lose your Etsy account, there is no getting it back.

Here are some examples of items that cannot be sold on Etsy:

Etsy's Intellectual Property Policy: Violating Intellectual Property on Etsy refers to the unauthorized use of copyrighted, trademarked, or patented material in the creation and sale of handmade items. This includes the use of logos, brand names, and other copyrighted material that are owned by third-party companies without permission.

Sellers violating intellectual property rights is by far the biggest problem on Etsy. You will see many products listed on Etsy that violate the copyright of brands. Disney, Marvel, Star Wars, Care Bears, Stranger Things, and every single popular movie, television show, and celebrity are all illegally reproduced every single day on Etsy.

Arguably the biggest area of intellectual property infringement on Etsy is counterfeit Disney products. If a seller is using Disney's trademarked characters, logos, movie titles, theme park graphics, and even song lyrics in their handmade items without express written permission from Disney, they are violating Disney's intellectual property rights. Disney holds exclusive rights to the use of their movies, music, characters, parks, and merchandise. Any unauthorized use is considered trademark infringement. This doesn't just apply to the word "Disney" but to all of their images, including the outline of Mickey Mouse's ears and the various princess castles.

So how are these products even for sale on Etsy in the first place? The fact is that Etsy will not usually take down items that violate copyright. Instead, they will wait for the copyright holder to notify them of illegal listings. That's right: It takes Disney going through Etsy's website and telling Etsy which listings are illegal. Only then will Etsy remove the listings and in some cases terminate the seller's account.

Now I know what you may be thinking: "If everyone else is doing it, maybe I can get away with it, too." And you may be able to sell counterfeit products for a while and even make a nice profit. But once your account gets flagged and your items are taken down, any attempt by you to relist them on Etsy or another website may result in Disney or whatever company holding the trademark you used filing a lawsuit against you.

And yes, Disney has sued crafters who have made counterfeit Disney products, including mouse ears and clothing.

Just because some people may be getting away with it for a while, I'm not risking my business and personal finances to profit off knock-off Disney products!

Disney, is, of course, a well-known brand. But how can you check for sure if an image, saying, or product is trademarked? Fortunately, there is a free website where you can research trademarks. The States Patent and Trademark Office (USPTO) website is the official website for searching for and registering trademarks in the United States.

To search for a trademark, visit the USPTO's Trademark Electronic Search System (TESS) at uspto.com. From there, you can search for trademarks using various search criteria, such as the name of the trademark owner, the trademark itself, or the registration number.

It's important to note that the USPTO's database may not include all trademarks, as there may be common law trademarks that are not registered with the USPTO. Therefore, if you are unsure whether an item or design may violate a trademark, it may be best to consult with a legal professional or trademark attorney for guidance.

My rule of thumb is that if someone else made it, it cannot be used. If someone else created it, wrote it, sang it, drew it, or developed it in any way shape, or form, it is their intellectual property and cannot be used in the creation of handmade items to sell, whether on Etsy or at a local craft show. This includes all movies, television shows, books, music, brands, and even celebrities themselves. That means no Disney tee shirts, no Taylor Swift tote bags, and no toys modeled after Star Wars characters. Again, even though you will see these products for sale on Etsy, eventually the companies that hold the trademark will come along and force Etsy to pull your listing.

Or worse, they will sue you for copyright infringement.

Illegal items: Illegal Items to sell or possess, such as drugs, weapons, and stolen goods, cannot be sold on Etsy. Using images of these products on things such as clothing and stickers is also prohibited.

Hazardous Materials: Items that pose a safety risk, such as explosives, firearms, and chemicals, are not allowed to be sold on Etsy.

Prohibited Items: Certain items are prohibited on Etsy, including live animals, human remains, prescription drugs, medical devices, tobacco, vaping products, lottery items, and alcohol. You cannot sell items that promote hate speech or discrimination. And you also cannot sell items that are considered pornographic or have adult content.

Reselling of Mass-Produced Items: While vintage items and craft supplies can be sold on Etsy, sellers are not allowed to sell mass-produced items or items that they did not make themselves. For example, you can sell doll parts that you make yourself, are vintage, or that you purchased at a retail store or from a wholesale company. However, you can't sell dolls on Etsy that you bought in the toy aisle at Walmart.

For example, if you make clothes for Barbie dolls, not only can you not sell new Barbie dolls themselves, but you can't use the word "Barbie" anywhere in the listing as "Barbie" is a trademarked brand. An exception would be if you made handmade clothing for *vintage* Barbie dolls. In this case, since the doll is vintage, you can sell it on Etsy along with any handmade clothing. Otherwise, you would need to list clothing as fitting 11.5" dolls. You could use a Barbie doll to model the clothes in your photos, but you cannot use the words "Barbie" or "Mattel."

So, no illegal, hazardous, prohibited, or mass-produced items can be sold on Etsy. But what types of handmade items CAN you sell on Etsy?

According to Etsy's 2021 Q4 financial report, the top-selling categories on Etsy in terms of Gross Merchandise Sales (GMS) were:

1. Home & Living
2. Jewelry & Accessories
3. Craft Supplies & Tools
4. Clothing & Shoes
5. Weddings

In terms of specific crafts within these categories, some of the most popular handmade items on Etsy include (in no particular order):

- Handmade jewelry, such as personalized necklaces and earrings
- Handmade home decor, such as hand-painted signs and customized doormats
- Handmade clothing and accessories, such as knit hats and scarves and hand-sewn tote bags
- Craft supplies and tools, such as yarn, beads, and fabric
- Wedding accessories, such as personalized wedding favors and handcrafted wedding invitations
- Children's toys including those made from wood or yarn
- Baby items including clothing and accessories, nursery décor, and teething toys
- Beauty products including handmade scrubs and lotions
- Candles, food, and even pet treats

Don't see your particular handmade items listed above? Don't worry! These are just some examples of the types of crafts popular on Etsy. The fact is that there are an unlimited number of handmade items that you can sell. As long as your crafts aren't in violation of any of Etsy's policies, if you are making it, you can likely sell it!

Checking out the competition is natural for any business, and selling on Etsy is no different. Remember that you never, ever want to copy another seller's products. But you can take inspiration from the top Etsy sellers. Look at not only the products they sell but how they present them in their photos and listing descriptions. Study their shop policies and how they handle shipping. They've made it to the top for a reason, so take note of what they are doing and see what strategies of theirs that you can implement into your shop.

There are hundreds of thousands of artisans selling their wares on Etsy. Here is just a sampling of the top shops:

- Caitlyn Minimalist: Custom handmade jewelry
- ModParty: Custom bridesmaid's gifts and favors for weddings, birthdays, and baby showers
- Pint Sized Premium: Handmade baby onesies and toddler tees
- Silver Rain Silver: Handmade sterling silver jewelry
- Spoon Flower: Custom handmade fabric and wallpaper
- Tara Sparkes Tumblers: Digital downloads of tumbler wraps for water bottles
- Twist Stationery: Custom greeting cards and invitations
- Warung Beads: Seller of jewelry-making supplies
- World Incense Store: Crystals, tumbled stones, jewelry, and candles

Customization: While most crafters sell their wares as-is, there is another opportunity to make money on Etsy and that is by offering customization. This means that buyers can request specific details or modifications to the item, such as adding a name, choosing the color, or picking from several size options.

When creating a listing for a handmade item on Etsy, sellers can choose to include customization options in the listing. They can specify what types of customizations they are willing to make, and buyers can select from these options when placing their orders.

Etsy also provides tools to help sellers manage custom orders, such as the ability to communicate with buyers to discuss their specific requests, and the ability to create custom listings for unique items.

Shipping: The only real issue you may face when it comes to selling your crafts on Etsy is shipping large or extremely delicate items. Handmade items that are oversized or fragile may require special packaging or shipping methods to ensure they arrive at their destination safely and undamaged.

Large items, such as furniture or artwork, usually require freight shipping or white-glove delivery services, which are more expensive and time-consuming than standard shipping methods. Additionally, shipping delicate items, such as glassware or ceramics, requires careful packaging and investment in packing peanuts and bubble wrap to prevent damage during transit.

I will walk you through the process of shipping orders later in this book. But for now, consider focusing on selling small items first. Once you get the hang of shipping, you can start to add larger and more fragile items to your shop if you create those.

Research: If you have an interest in selling crafts online but haven't started creating any items yet, or if you have some items but are unsure of their demand on platforms like Etsy, there are some steps you can take to research and analyze the market. Note that what sells well in your local area may be oversaturated on Etsy. Selling online may require you to narrow down your niche, expand your product line, or both.

One way to start your research is to visit Etsy.com and search for the type of craft you are interested in selling. This will give you a good idea of the top-selling items and the most successful shops on the platform. By taking a look at the top handmade shops, you can compare your potential products with theirs and identify potential gaps in the market that you can fill with your unique items. This might mean finding a niche that they haven't covered yet or introducing something entirely new to the market. Look at their pricing, product descriptions, and photographs. You can use this information to improve your product listings and stand out from the competition.

Aside from Etsy itself, there are also several third-party research tools available that can help you in your market analysis. For instance, websites like EtsyCheck and eRank can provide you with valuable insights into trending products and popular searches on the platform. By using these tools, you can find the voids in the marketplace that you can fill with your products.

For example, if you search for the keyword "handmade gifts" on EtsyCheck or eRank, you may see that this is a highly competitive market. However, by delving deeper into the analytics, you will discover that specific types of handmade gifts such as "handmade soap gift sets" or "handmade gift boxes for men" are highly searched but have low competition. This information can help you narrow down your product offerings and cater to the demands of your potential customers.

Another way to research is to check out social media platforms like Instagram and Pinterest, which are great sources of inspiration for handmade items and are where you will find avid makers and craft shoppers. You can browse through hashtags related to your craft and see what other people are creating. This can give you ideas for your products and help you stay up-to-date with the latest trends.

Remember that when you sell on Etsy, you have access to customers around the world. If you have found that your handmade items aren't selling well in your local area, you just might find the audience for them on Etsy. If the crafts you make are oversaturated on Etsy, you can find ways to narrow your focus and fill in holes in the market. Seek out the underserved niches and adjust your products to target those markets.

For the Beginner: If you are new to crafting and are intrigued by the idea of selling handmade items on Etsy but have no idea where to start, the following are some ideas. All of these crafts can be self-taught using books, kits, and YouTube videos. Browse the DIY kit sets at Barnes & Noble, Michael's, Hobby Lobby, JoAnn Fabrics, and the big box stores for beginner kits that will teach you the basics. A simple YouTube search for whatever craft you are thinking about will likely bring up hundreds if not thousands of results.

- **Handmade greeting cards:** You can create beautiful and unique greeting cards using various techniques like stamping, embossing, or watercolor painting. Stamping is the easiest way to create these cards, and you can try adding embellishments such as glitter or 3D elements. By utilizing card stock, which is available at any craft store, you can make greeting cards to sell in singles or sets.
- **Jewelry:** You can make simple and elegant jewelry pieces like earrings, bracelets, and necklaces using beads, wire, or polymer clay. There are plenty of tutorials available online to help you get started and you can find jewelry-making kits at every craft and big box store. Creating beaded bracelets is the easiest place to start when it comes to making jewelry, followed by earrings and necklaces.
- **Knit or crochet scarves and hats:** These are popular items on Etsy, and they are relatively easy to make even for beginners. There are numerous kits on the market as well as

thousands of YouTube tutorials. You can experiment with different yarn colors and textures to create unique designs that aren't already being sold on Etsy.

- **Candles:** You can make candles using natural wax, essential oils, and fragrances. These can be sold in various sizes and scents and make great gifts. You can buy candle kits in stores and online. By experimenting with different scents and packaging, you can easily make candles that are unique to the market.
- **Tote bags:** You can create personalized tote bags using fabric paint or iron-on transfers. These are versatile and can be used for grocery shopping, carrying books, or as a beach bag. You can purchase blank canvas tote bags in stores and online as well as ready-to-use iron-on transfers.
- **Bath bombs:** You can make bath bombs using natural ingredients like baking soda, citric acid, and essential oils. These are popular items on Etsy and can be sold in various scents and shapes.
- **Gift baskets:** You can put together gift baskets or boxes using pre-made items. Because putting together these packages fall under the umbrella of being "handmade," it's okay to use products you purchase at retail or wholesale. From food baskets to get-well boxes, there are endless designs you can make.
- **Party favors:** These days it isn't a party without custom favors for the guests. From small food gifts to large "swag" bags, party favors, like gift baskets, can be assembled with pre-made materials.
- **Baked goods:** Etsy allows for the sale of bakery products, homemade candies, and other foods. If you love to bake, you can find a ready supply of shoppers eager to buy treats.

Never Stop Learning: Whatever you decide to sell on Etsy, it's important to keep up to date with trends. Boho and botanical might be in one year but bright and modern could be in demand the next. While you don't want to sacrifice your art for the sake of making sales, you are, after all, running a business. Finding the sweet spot between what you are happy creating and what customers are shopping for is what separates the top shops from the rest. Trends and tastes change. To be successful, you need to change with them.

CHAPTER THREE: OPENING AN ETSY SHOP

So far we have discussed the benefits of expanding your crafting business to Etsy and the various handmade items you can sell (and not sell) on the platform. Assuming you have products ready to sell, the next step is to create a seller account and set up your Etsy shop. This chapter will walk you step by step through the entire process.

If you're already an Etsy shopper, creating a seller account is an additional process that requires additional information for approval to sell products. You will still be logged in under your buyer account, so there will be no need to switch back and forth between the two.

To set up an Etsy seller account, follow these steps:

1. Go to the **Etsy website** and click on the **Sell on Etsy** button.
2. Click the **Open your Etsy shop** button.
3. Enter your **email address** and **password** to create an account or sign in with an existing account. You can create your seller account under your buyer account, you'll just need to add some additional information.
4. Choose your **shop language** and **country**.
5. Enter your **shop name.**
6. Agree to **Etsy's terms of use and policies.**
7. Click the **Create your shop** button to complete the process.

Once you've completed the **Create Your Etsy Shop** process, the next step is to configure your **Shop Preferences**. You can easily access the **Shop Manager** by clicking on the store-shaped icon located at the top of all Etsy pages in your **Etsy Seller Dashboard**. Keep in mind that you have the option to skip this step and return later to set up your shop preferences. Additionally, you can modify your settings at any time in the future.

PRO TIP: I have my **Shop Manager** bookmarked on my desktop computer so that I can quickly access it to create new listings and manage my shop. I also have the **Etsy Seller App** installed on my phone so I can easily access my account from anywhere at any time. Being able to access my shop when I'm away from my office is important as it allows me to quickly answer any messages from buyers. Etsy is very strict about sellers answering questions from customers as quickly as possible; failing to do so in a timely manner can affect your seller status. So having the app allows me to respond to questions even when I am away from my office.

Etsy Shop Preferences are the settings that allow you to customize and manage various aspects of your Etsy shop. You can access your shop preferences by going to **Shop Manager** and clicking on the **Preferences** tab.

Here are some of the things you can do in your **Etsy Shop Preferences**:

- Set your shop location and language.
- Set your shop policies, such as your return policy.
- Customize your shop's appearance by adding a banner image, logo, and other branding elements.
- Enable automatic renewal for your listings.
- Choose how you want to handle orders, including setting up automatic email responses.
- Set up Google Analytics to track your shop's performance.
- Set up shipping profiles to streamline the process of shipping your products.
- Enable or disable various features, such as the ability to offer gift wrapping or to allow customers to request custom orders.

Time Commitment: When you set up your shop on Etsy, they will ask you how much time you plan to dedicate to it. This is just a way for them to understand how serious you are about being a seller, but don't worry, it won't make or break your ability to sell successfully on Etsy. You have the option to select if selling on Etsy is your full-time or part-time gig, or you can skip the question altogether.

Shop Name: Selecting the name for your Etsy shop sets the tone for your business. It's one of the first things potential customers will see when they stumble across your store, so you want to make sure it's eye-catching, memorable, and accurately reflects your brand.

If you're already running a local craft business, you may already have a name that you're happy with. However, if someone else on Etsy is already using that name, you will have to create a different one. Search Etsy for the name you want to see what comes up. If yours is already taken, you can modify yours slightly. For instance, if your business is called "Cassie's Candles" and that name is taken, you could name your shop "Cassie's Candle Shop" or Cassie's Candle Shoppe."

You need to make sure that your shop name adheres to Etsy's naming guidelines and that it doesn't contain any prohibited words or phrases. Etsy has certain requirements and guidelines for shop names to ensure that they are appropriate and do not violate the platform's policies. Here are some of the main requirements and guidelines for shop names on Etsy:

- Shop names must be unique and not already in use by another Etsy seller.
- Shop names must not contain any prohibited words or phrases, such as offensive language or trademarked terms.
- Shop names must not imply that you are affiliated with Etsy or any other company or organization.
- Shop names must not contain any personal information, such

as phone numbers or addresses.

- Shop names must not be too long or difficult to spell or pronounce.

- Shop names must be 4-20 characters in length.
- Shop names cannot contain spaces or special characters.
- Shop names cannot contain profanity.
- Shop names cannot infringe on another's trademark.

Set Up Payment & Billing: In the next step of setting up your Etsy shop, you will be required to provide payment and billing information. This includes entering a valid payment method that Etsy can use to charge you in case your fees exceed your sales.

Remember that when you sell something on Etsy, Etsy will automatically take out their fees and shipping costs before depositing the remaining balance in your Etsy account. If you have to process a refund or if your fees exceed your net profits, your Etsy balance could fall into the negative. At that time, Etsy would charge your credit card for any outstanding fees you've occurred.

When setting up your Etsy shop, you will also need to specify a payment method so Etsy can pay you for your sales. To set up your Etsy shop's payment and billing, you will need to follow these steps:

1. Go to the **Shop Manager** and click on the **Finances** tab.
2. Etsy will prompt you to enter your bank account routing information for direct deposit.
3. Choose your **Deposit schedule** (every day, once a week, every two weeks, or once a month)
4. Click the **Save** button to save your payment settings.

The information you need to provide to set up an Etsy seller account varies depending on the country you are registering in as well as if you are signing up as an individual/sole proprietorship or a business entity. If you're registering as an individual/sole proprietor, you will be required to furnish personal details like your name, contact information, and, if you're located in the United States, your social security number. On the other hand, if you're registering a business, specifically an LLC, you will need to provide more extensive information about your enterprise, such as its official name, contact information, and pertinent documentation.

Are you confused about the difference between a sole proprietorship and an LLC? Don't worry, many new sellers are. Here is an explanation of the difference between them:

A **sole proprietorship** is a business entity in which an individual is the sole owner and operator of the business. As a sole proprietor, the business owner has complete control over all aspects of their business and is personally responsible for all debts and liabilities. For tax purposes, the business is not considered a separate entity, and the owner reports all business income and expenses on their tax return. In the United States, a sole proprietor may use their Social Security number as their business identification number for tax purposes.

A **Limited Liability Company,** usually referred to as an **LLC,** also offers greater flexibility in terms of taxation. By default, an LLC is considered a "pass-through" entity, which means that the profits and losses of the business pass through to the owners' personal tax returns, and the business itself does not pay federal income taxes. However, LLCs can choose to be taxed as a corporation if they prefer.

Unlike a sole proprietorship, an LLC can have an unlimited number of owners. In terms of legal requirements, an LLC typically requires more paperwork and formalities than a sole proprietorship. This can include filing articles of organization with the state, creating an operating agreement, and obtaining any necessary licenses or permits. However, the exact requirements vary by state.

Most Etsy sellers, including myself, are sole proprietors. As explained above, being a sole proprietor simply means that I pay taxes as an individual, not a corporation, using my social security number and not a business license. I operate my Etsy shop as a one-person business and am not registered as a corporation or LLC with the government. As a sole proprietorship, I pay taxes (in America) as an individual using my social security number and do not need a business license.

Note that the need for a business license varies by location; be sure to consult your county or with a local tax professional or CPA to learn the laws for your area.

When registering your business on Etsy, you will need to provide specific information on the **How you'll get paid** page during the setup process of your shop, including:

- Your full legal name and contact information including address and phone number
- Your social security number (for United States citizens) or your taxpayer identification number (TIN)
- Your bank account information, including the bank name, routing number, and account number. You can find your routing and account numbers at the bottom of your checks.

Test Deposit: After you have provided your payment and billing information, Etsy may initiate a "test deposit," which is simply a verification process to ensure the accuracy of your payment information and to confirm that you can receive payouts. This process involves Etsy issuing you a small deposit, typically less than a dollar, to your bank account. You are not required to repay this test deposit.

To complete the verification process, you will need to check your bank account to locate the test deposit and confirm that you have received it. Once you have done so, you simply enter the amount of the test deposit on the *How you'll get paid* page to finalize the verification process. Note that Etsy will remind you to complete this process and give you prompts to do so.

The test deposit may take a few days to appear in your account, so be sure to check back periodically if you do not see it right away. If you have any issues with the verification process, you can contact Etsy's support team for assistance. You can easily contact Etsy support at any time and for any reason by following these steps:

1. Go to **www.etsy.com** and click the **Help & Policies** tab at the bottom of the page.
2. Scroll down to the **Contacting Etsy** section and click the **Contact Us** button.
3. Select the appropriate **category** for your issue from the dropdown menu.
4. Enter a **subject** and a **detailed description** of your issue in the provided fields.
5. Click the **Continue** button to submit your request.

Etsy support typically responds within 24 hours, although it can take longer during peak times.

Two-Factor Authentication: Two-factor authentication is an additional security measure that requires you to provide a verification code when signing in from an unrecognized browser or device. This helps to protect your account from unauthorized access and ensures that only you can access your Etsy shop. More and more businesses, including banks, social media platforms, and e-commerce websites are encouraging users to implement two-factor authentication to protect their accounts.

To set up two-factor authentication, you will need to choose a method for receiving your verification code. Etsy allows you to receive your verification code in one of three ways:

1. **Text message:** If you choose this option, you will receive a text message with your verification code whenever you need to sign in from an unrecognized browser or device.
2. **Authenticator app:** If you choose this option, you will need to download an authenticator app on your phone and use it to generate your verification code whenever you need to sign in from an unrecognized browser or device.
3. **Email:** If you choose this option, you will receive an email with your verification code whenever you need to sign in from an unrecognized browser or device.

Set Up Your Storefront: Once you've gotten through entering your personal and banking information, verifying your account, and setting up two-factor authorization, you can move on to the fun step of designing your Etsy shop storefront!

To set up your Etsy shop storefront, follow these steps (note that we'll go over these options more in-depth later in this chapter):

1. Go to your Etsy seller dashboard and click the **Shop settings** tab.
2. Click the **Shop info & Appearance** tab on the left side of the page.
3. Enter a **shop title** and **shop announcement** that will appear at the top of your shop's homepage.
4. Add a **shop banner** image that will appear at the top of your

shop's homepage.

5. Add a **shop icon**, which is a small image that will represent your shop on Etsy.
6. Enter a **shop description** that will appear on your shop's homepage and in search results.
7. Click the **Save** button to save your changes.

Etsy Standard: *Etsy Standard* is the default level of shop access for all sellers on the platform. It offers all of the basic features and functions necessary for selling on Etsy. There is no additional charge to open an Etsy shop; the only upfront cost is the listing fee of $0.20 per item, charged when you create a new listing or relist an expired one. The fee covers four months, meaning you can list one item on Etsy for one year for only $.80. Remember that final value fees apply once an item sells, but those fees are automatically deducted from your balance along with postage costs if you print your shipping labels through Etsy.

To edit your Etsy Shop, log into your **Shop Manager**. Then **click on the pencil icon next to your shop's name**. This will bring up the page where you can edit your shop's banner, icon, and featured items area.

Etsy Plus: *Etsy Plus* is a subscription shop plan that provides sellers with advanced features and tools beyond what is included in the basic *Etsy Standard* plan. For a monthly fee of $10, *Etsy Plus* members receive listing 15 credits and $5 in credit towards *Etsy Ads*.

In addition to these advertising benefits, *Etsy Plus* subscribers get access to advanced shop appearance options, a custom domain name, and Etsy's wholesale platform. Moreover, *Etsy Plus* offers a discount on Hover domains, although sellers can choose to purchase a domain from other providers such as GoDaddy.

Once you have settled on your business name, I recommend locking the domain name in before someone else claims it. I own the domains for several variations of my name, all of which point to my Amazon Author Page where my books are located.

Etsy Plus subscribers have the option to enable *Restock requests* in their listings, which allows the shopper to view your sold-out listings and to sign up to receive an alert when items are back in stock. And finally, Etsy Plus subscribers have access to discounts and perks such as savings on custom shipping boxes, business cards, and other promotional materials.

Featured Items: Featured items are listings or shop sections that are prominently displayed on a seller's shop page. All sellers on Etsy have the **standard grid** option, which allows you to feature up to four listings or shop sections on your shop's page.

Etsy Plus subscribers have the additional option to use a **mixed grid layout.** With a mixed grid layout, *Etsy Plus* subscribers can feature one big listing or shop section along with four smaller items or shop sections on their shop page.

While you do not have to enable these grid options, if you do, be sure to carefully select the items or sections you want to feature as they will be the first thing buyers see when they visit your Etsy shop. Make sure you keep them up to date and in season. For example, if you selected Christmas items to be highlighted during the holiday season, don't forget to change them out after December 25th. Leaving up outdated featured items gives the appearance that you don't care about your shop, which can make customers think you won't care about their orders. It is better not to use grids than to leave stale arrangements up.

Should you start your Etsy shop with *Etsy Standard* or upgrade to *Etsy Plus*? That is a choice only you can make. Most sellers start with *Etsy Standard* and then upgrade to *Etsy Plus* as their business grows. The listing and ad credits, the customization options, the advanced shop management, the promotional tools, and the priority customer support are, in my opinion, all well worth the $10 monthly fee. And since you pay on a month-to-month basis, you can cancel your subscription at any time and revert to *Etsy Standard*.

When you sell online, regardless of the platform you sell on or what items you sell, having as many items listed as possible will give you the best chance of making sales. If you only make one handmade item in one design, it will be hard to make sales on Etsy. However, by offering as many different options as possible, you will have an easier time attracting buyers. Again, it only costs $.80 to list an item for one year on Etsy, which means you could list 100 items for only $80 for a year. That's likely the same or less than you are paying to have a booth at just one local craft show!

Etsy Shop Icon: Your Etsy shop icon, also known as your logo or profile picture, is a small image that serves as the visual representation of your shop on the Etsy platform. It appears alongside your shop name on your shop's homepage, on your listings, and various other pages on the Etsy website and app.

Your shop icon is a crucial component of your branding and should ideally be used across all your social media platforms to maintain consistency and brand recognition. This means that your Etsy shop icon should be the same profile picture on every website where your business has a presence. This will make it easier for customers to recognize your brand on whatever platform they are on. Since some online sellers have similar names, sometimes it's the profile picture that will end up separating you from other businesses when people are searching for you online.

To set up your **Etsy shop icon**, you will need to follow these steps:

1. Sign into your Etsy account and go to the **Shop Manager**

section.

2. Click on **Settings** and then click on the **Info & Appearance** tab.
3. Scroll down to the **Shop Icon** section and click on the **Change Icon** button.
4. Select the image you want to use as your shop icon from your computer or device. The image must be at least 500 x 500 pixels and in a .jpg, .gif, or .png format.
5. Click on the **Save** button to apply your changes.

Shop Story: An **Etsy shop story** is where you can share a summary of your shop's products, your overall brand, your business goals, and a bit about you as a person. Connecting with shoppers in this way shows them you are a real person, which can go a long way toward making a more personal connection with your customers.

To set up your **Etsy shop story** follow these steps:

1. Sign into your Etsy account and click on the **Shop Manager** button in the top right corner of the page.
2. Click on the **Settings** tab and then click on the **About Your Shop** tab.
3. Click on the **Story tab** at the top of the page.
4. Enter in a **Story Headline.**
5. Fill in the **Story** field.
6. You can also add a **Shop Video** here.
7. You can also add in **Shop Photos.**
8. You can also **add links to your social media pages.**
9. Click on the **Save** button to apply your changes.
10. You can edit or delete any of these sections any time after you create them.

Etsy Shop Title & Shop Announcement: The *Shop Title* and *Shop Announcement* are important parts of your Etsy shop's storefront as they appear at the top of your shop's homepage, meaning they are the first sections customers will see when visiting your shop.

Your *Shop Title* should be a short phrase that represents your store and the products you offer. On the other hand, your *Shop Announcement* is a brief message that can be used to share important time-sensitive information with your customers, such as new product launches, promotions, or updated policies. Both of these fields are optional.

To create a *Shop Title,* choose a phrase that accurately reflects your shop's products and style. My Shop Title is *Retro & Vintage Inspired Stickers & Magnets.* For the *Shop Announcement,* craft a message that is informative and engaging, and consider adding relevant keywords to maximize your Etsy SEO. My *Shop Announcement* is *Welcome to Jean Lee Publishing! We specialize in vinyl waterproof stickers and magnets that are perfect for water bottles, laptops, refrigerators, cars, crafting, and gifting. All items ship for FREE from Iowa the following business day after orders are placed, with USPS tracking immediately uploaded for your convenience.*

To access your *Shop Title* and *Shop Announcement* sections, click on the **Settings** tab in your **Shop Manager** and then click on **Info & Appearance.** You can change these areas at any time or leave them blank until you have built up your shop and are more comfortable filling them out.

Message to Buyers: Also under the *Info & Appearance* section is a space to write a message to your buyers that Etsy will automatically include on receipt pages and in the email they send to buyers whenever they place an order on the site. A simple "thank you for your order" message with a general statement about shipping is enough to include here, although this is an optional field. My message reads, *Thank you for your* *order! We appreciate your business! The tracking information has been uploaded for your convenience.*

Message to Buyers for Digital Items: Also under the *Info & Appearance* section is a space to write a message to buyers for digital items such as printables that customers can download and print out themselves. Etsy offers the following directions for this section: *If you sell digital items, we will include this message on the Downloads page for digital orders. It applies to all digital listings purchased from your shop.*

Etsy Shop Banner: An Etsy shop banner is a large image that appears at the top of your shop's homepage and gives potential customers an idea of what your shop is all about. Just as with your *Shop Title* and *Shop Announcement*, your banner image is an important element of your shop's appearance, as it helps create a professional and cohesive look for your shop. And while you don't have to have a shop banner, your shop will look much better with one.

To edit your Etsy Banner, first, log into your **Shop Manager**. Then **click on the pencil icon next to your shop's name,** which is under SALES CHANNELS on the left-hand side of the page. This will bring up a page where you can edit your shop's banner.

Just as you want your Etsy shop icon to be cohesive across all of your social media platforms, you want to do the same with your banner. Facebook and YouTube both allow banners, and it's easy to place your Etsy banner on both of those sites. You can create a banner using Canva or pay to have one created for you on a site such as Fiverr or UpWork.

Etsy Plus subscribers have access to four different banner styles:

- **Carousel** allows you to show off multiple photos, one at a time, which you can link to listings or sections.
- **Collage** allows you to combine up to four photos in a

collage.

- **Big Banner** allows you to fill the top of your shop with one image that you can link to a listing or section.
- **Mini Banner** allows you to add a visual pop while keeping the focus on your listings.

Mixed Grid: All Etsy shops have the option to use a *Standard Grid* but *Etsy Plus* shops can also choose a *Mixed Grid* option that features five listings or shop sections with a couple of layout choices.

To edit your grid options, first, log into your **Shop Manager**. Then **click on the pencil icon next to your shop's name**. This will bring up a page where you can edit your shop's **Featured Items** with your grid options. Some sellers change their grid options every day to ensure returning customers are always greeted with a new look. However, most sellers opt to change them once a week or once a month.

Hiring Out Design Services: When building your brand on Etsy, you want to use consistent graphics across not only your shop but all of your social media platforms to create a cohesive brand image. If you aren't able to design your logos and banners yourself, or you simply don't have the time to create them, you can hire graphic designers to do the work for you.

There are several places where you can hire a designer to create your Etsy shop logo and banners, along with all graphics for your social media pages. Some options include:

1. **Fiverr:** Fiverr is an online marketplace where you can find freelance designers who offer a wide range of design services, including logo and banner design. You can browse through portfolios and reviews to find a designer who meets your needs and budget. It's easy to find a designer for under $10, especially new designers on the site who are eager to build

their portfolios. I recommend choosing designers that offer at least two revisions of your order to ensure you get exactly what you want. A simple search of the "Etsy logo" or "Etsy banner" will get you started in your search.

2. **Upwork:** Upwork is another online marketplace where you can find freelance designers for hire. You can post a job listing and receive proposals from designers who are interested in working with you. You will likely pay more for a designer on UpWork versus Fiverr, but the quality may also be better. Just like new designers on Fiverr charge less, you may find new designers on UpWork who are willing to do the job for less money to build their portfolio. As with Fiverr, I recommend choosing designers that offer at least two revisions. And try to find a designer who offers packages where you can get not only your Etsy graphics but all of the graphics you will need for your social media pages.

3. **99designs:** 99designs is a design contest platform where you can hold a design contest to receive multiple design options for your logo, icons, and banners. You can choose the design you like best and work with the designer to make any necessary revisions.

4. **Etsy:** You can also find designers on Etsy who offer design services, including logo and banner design.

5. **Friends & Family:** You can seek your local graphic design recommendations on Facebook. You never know who your friends and family may now that do the kind of work you are looking to hire out.

Shop Options: You can find **Options** under the **Settings** tab in your shop managers. Etsy allows you to pre-determine several options for your store, including:

Rearrange Your Shop: Enabling this feature will show shop visitors the *Custom* sort option by default. Or you can disable this feature so that shop visitors will see the *Most Recently Listed* sort option by default.

Custom Order Requests: If you are offering custom or personalized products, you can enable a setting where a *Request Custom Order* button will appear across your shop. If you do not offer personalized items, you will want to disable this feature so customers know that the products you are selling are as pictured. Note, however, that this won't stop some people from messaging you to ask if you offer personalization.

Offer Gift Wrapping: Etsy allows sellers to offer gift wrapping services to their buyers. Think long and hard before offering gift wrap as customers will expect items to be wrapped as they would be in a luxury department store setting. Wrapping items will add time to your process, and many crafted items require special size boxes, which adds more to the cost.

However, if you do want to offer gift wrapping, Etsy allows you to set your price for buyers to pay. Your gift options will then appear on every listing (except for digital products). I have never offered gift wrapping. When buyers ask, I simply explain that to ensure their items arrive safely that I do not gift wrap them but rather take care in packaging them with clean packing materials.

Offer Gift Message: While gift wrapping can be a costly and time-consuming service, enabling the ability for customers to offer a gift message with their order is free and easy to do. If your buyer chooses to include a gift message, it will print on a sheet of paper that you can fold into a gift card. Note that if a customer includes a gift message that the packing slip will print without the price of the item showing.

PRO TIP: Sometimes customers will contact you after they have paid for the order and ask you to send the package to a different address. Maybe they forgot to update their address or they want it sent as a gift. Note that if you change the address, the order will no longer qualify for Etsy Seller Protection. I will offer to cancel the order and ask the customer to repurchase it with the correct shipping address.

Automatic Listing Translation: Even if you only plan to sell items within your own country, such as America, it's important to note that not all shoppers are native speakers. Enabling Etsy to automatically translate your listing titles and descriptions into the buyer's designated language is a free and easy way to expand your customer base. English my be the official language of the United States, but there are numerous Spanish speakers in our country along with immigrants from all over the world. Enabling language translations makes it easier for more people to shop from your store.

Sold Listings: You can choose to let other Etsy users see your sold listings, or you can hide them. Some sellers choose to hide their sold listings for fear that other sellers will see and then steal their best-selling designs. I let users see my sold listings so that customers can see my most popular items, which might help them decide to purchase them, too. The choice to show or hide your sold listings is entirely up to you. If you choose to show them but later want to hide them, you can easily edit this section.

Current Time Zone: You can set your shop's time zone here. This is helpful when you are shipping orders as it lets customers know where you are located in relation to them so that they will have a better idea of how long shipping may take. It also helps let customers know why you may be taking a while to answer their message. After all, it might be daytime for them but a night for you.

Vacation Mode: If you ever need to put your Etsy shop on vacation (whether because you are taking an actual vacation or are simply unable to process orders), you can easily put your entire store on vacation so that customers cannot purchase anything from your store. In fact, while your storefront will still be visible, your listings will be hidden. You can also include a *Vacation Announcement* that will display at the top of your shop. And you can write up a *Messages Autoreply*, which will be sent to anyone who sends you a message while your *Vacation Mode* is on.

It's good to know how to quickly put your shop on vacation not only on your computer but also on your smartphone in case of an emergency and to make sure someone close to you knows how to, as well. The last thing you want is for orders to pile up unfulfilled, which will cause Etsy to eventually cancel those orders, issue refunds to your customers, and put a strike against your account. I've had situations where I was in the hospital emergency room and had to use my phone to put my store on vacation.

Web Analytics: Etsy partners with Google to provide sellers with data regarding the volume of shop traffic and the sources of the traffic. You need to sign up for a free Google Analytics account to access this information.

Download Data: The *Download Data* section in your Etsy Seller Dashboard allows you to download various types of data about your Etsy shop in CSV (Comma Separated Value) format. Here is a breakdown of the different options available:

1. **Orders:** This option allows you to download data about your shop's orders, including order ID, date, buyer information, order status, and item details.
2. **Listings:** This option allows you to download data about your shop's listings, including listing ID, title, description,

price, quantity, and other relevant details.

3. **Finances:** This option allows you to download data about your shop's finances, including revenue, fees, taxes, and payment information.

4. **Shop:** This option allows you to download data about your shop's settings and preferences, including shop names, policies, and shipping information.

5. **Web Analytics:** This option allows you to download data about your shop's web analytics, including visits, views, conversion rates, revenue, traffic sources, and search terms.

By downloading this data, you can analyze it using spreadsheet software like Microsoft Excel or Google Sheets and gain deeper insights into your shop's performance. You can also use this data to create custom reports and visualizations that can help you make informed decisions about how to optimize your shop and drive more sales. Knowing where traffic is coming from tells you where you need to focus your marketing efforts. If you get a steady stream of customers from Etsy but not your social media accounts, you will know you need to work on building those sites up.

Close Shop: Also under the *Options* section is a tab to close your Etsy shop. Note that if you have *Etsy Standard,* you only pay when you list an item. So, there is no reason to close your shop if you simply aren't listing new products. If you have an *Etsy Plus* account, you can simply cancel that subscription and leave your shop as is, even if there are no listings, just in case you want to come back to it in the future. Remember that you can change the name of your shop at any time, so if you rebrand, you can easily change the name, look, and policies to fit a different business model.

Shipping Policies: The shipping settings section of your Etsy account (accessible under the **Settings** tab) is where you can manage and configure the shipping options for your shop. Note that you can create shipping profiles within each of your listings to match up with the various products you are selling. We'll be covering shipping in depth later in this book.

Policy Settings: Also under the Settings section is where you can create your Policy Settings. Here you can set up the following:

Returns & Exchanges: Etsy allows sellers to set their own policies for returns and exchanges on their products. Most sellers of handmade items do not allow for returns or exchanges unless an item is defective. Because you will likely be making products to order, it's difficult to absorb the costs of returns simply because someone changed their mind.

However, note that if you made a mistake on your end when creating the product you will have to accept a return. If a customer contacts me to let me know that I made a mistake with their order, I almost always just issue them a refund and allow them to keep the item so that I don't have to pay for the return shipping.

Cancellations: The cancellations setting on Etsy allows sellers to set their policies for canceling orders. These policies can vary from seller to seller and can include information on the conditions under which a buyer can cancel an order and any fees that may be associated with the cancellation.

It is considered good customer service to allow customers to cancel an order shortly after they place it. Sometimes a buyer may have simply made a mistake and will contact you within minutes of placing their order. I personally just agree to cancel these orders. Setting a timeframe for which you will accept cancellations is important to let buyers know they have a short window of time to request a cancellation. This is especially important if you make custom products that you only start producing once an order is placed.

Privacy: The privacy settings on Etsy allow users to control how their personal information is collected, used, and shared on the platform. These settings include options for controlling the types of information that is shared with Etsy and third-party partners, as well as options for managing communication preferences and account settings. In the privacy settings, users can choose to limit the types of information that Etsy collects from them, such as browsing data or search queries.

Production Partners: As we discussed earlier in this book, if you're using a third-party to help create your handmade products, you'll need to disclose them as a *Production Partner* in your Etsy shop. For example, if you design jewelry and hire a company to mass-produce your designs, you'll need to add this company as a *Production Partner.* You have the option to keep the names of your *Production Partners* private, and buyers will only see a message that you utilize a third-party to help produce your items.

It's important to note that using craft supplies to make your items does not require you to add the brand of the supplies or the store where you bought them to the *Production Partners* section. For instance, if you make jewelry and buy your beads and supplies from Michael's, you don't have to add Michael's as a *Production Partner.* Craft supplies and stores are not considered *Production Partners.*

Offsite Ads: Also under the *Settings* section is *Offsite Ads.* Etsy *Offsite Ads* is a marketing tool offered by Etsy that allows sellers to advertise their products on external websites like Google, Facebook, Instagram, and Pinterest.

If you're a seller on Etsy and you sell less than $10,000 a year on the platform, you have the option to enroll in Etsy *Offsite Ads.* This is a marketing program that allows Etsy to create and manage ads for your products on external websites like Google and Facebook. If a buyer clicks on one of your ads and makes a purchase within 30 days, you'll be charged a fee based on a percentage of the sale.

However, if you sell more than $10,000 a year on Etsy, you will be automatically enrolled in Etsy *Offsite Ads* and cannot opt out of the program. This has upset some sellers who feel that they should have the choice to opt-out. It's important to note that with Etsy *Offsite Ads,* you only pay for an ad when it leads to a sale. This means that you don't have to pay for clicks or impressions, and you only pay when you make a sale as a direct result of the ad.

Facebook Shops: *Facebook Shops* is another feature under the *Settings* tab on the Etsy seller dashboard that enables you to connect your Etsy shop with your Facebook account and establish a store on Facebook. This will allow you to sell your products directly on Facebook, in addition to your Etsy shop.

When you connect your Etsy shop to Facebook, you can easily transfer your products, product information, and inventory to your Facebook store. Furthermore, once connected, you can sync your inventory and sales across both platforms, so you don't have to worry about managing stock levels or order fulfillment between the two.

It is important to note that you will need to have a Facebook page set up before creating a store and linking it to your Etsy shop. We will discuss creating a Facebook page for your business later in this book. Additionally, Facebook has certain policies and guidelines regarding the use of its platform for commerce, so make sure to familiarize yourself with them before utilizing *Facebook Shops.*

Community & Help: You can keep up with all of Etsy's announcements as well as get help under the *Community & Help* section, which is linked in your *Shop Manager.* You can also access the *Help Center* from any Etsy page directly on the site by scrolling down to the very bottom and locating the *Help* section.

Etsy Fees: We covered Etsy fees earlier in this book, but we must go over them again so you know how much money you will be spending to sell on the platform:

Listing Fees: Etsy charges a $.20 fee to list an item for four months. This $.20 fee is charged whenever you create a new listing or relist an expired one. Note that this fee is for one LISTING. You may list several items within one listing if you have different variations of it. For example, in my Etsy sticker shop, I sell matte stickers, holographic stickers, and magnets of the same design. I sometimes create one listing for each design but offer all three options under each listing. I don't pay for each variation. I only pay the $.20 fee for the single listing.

While no one likes to pay fees, the $.20 listing fee on Etsy is quite low, especially when compared to other e-commerce sites like Amazon or eBay. At the end of the four months, you can opt to renew the listing for another four months at the same cost of $0.20, making the total cost for one item to be listed for a full year only $0.80. You will find that listing on Etsy costs much less compared to the cost to rent booth space at craft shows!

Transaction Fees: In addition to the listing fee, Etsy also charges a transaction fee on each sale that you make. Like their low listing fees, this 5% transaction fee on Etsy is a small price to pay for the exposure and resources provided by the platform, including payment processing and file delivery. The fee is calculated on the sale price of each item, including shipping and gift-wrapping charges if there are any, and it helps cover the costs of running and maintaining the Etsy website.

Payment Processing Fees: Etsy makes it easy for customers to pay using a variety of methods as it partners with different payment processors to handle transactions, and these processors charge various fees for their services. This fee is typically around 2.9% + $.30 per transaction, which allows customers to pay for their orders using their debit cards, credit cards, or even PayPal. If you had to arrange payment processing yourself, it would cost much more. Not only does Etsy handle the payments from buyers, but they also handle the distribution of your profits to your bank account. When you sell your crafts on Etsy, you won't have to worry about having change to cash out customers!

Advertising & Promotional Fees: In addition to the listing and payment processing fees, Etsy offers various advertising and promotional options for sellers who want to increase the visibility of their products. These options come with additional fees, which vary depending on the specific advertising or promotion being used.

Etsy Ads: Just listing products for sale on Etsy may not be enough to get customers to find your items. That's where *Etsy Ads* come in. *Etsy Ads* is an advertising program that lets you promote your products right on the Etsy site.

To get started with *Etsy Ads,* just head to your **Seller Dashboard**, click on the **Marketing** tab, and select **Etsy Ads**. Keep in mind that you have to pay every time someone clicks on your ad, regardless of whether or not they make a purchase. If you want to test Etsy ads, I recommend starting with a $5 daily budget for a month to see how your ads perform. You can adjust your budget at any time to fit your needs or you can cancel the ad if you aren't seeing results.

Etsy Offsite Ads: Unlike regular *Etsy Ads*, which are only shown on Etsy and for which you have to pay every time someone clicks on your ad, *Etsy Offsite Ads* offer sellers a chance to expand their reach beyond the Etsy marketplace and potentially increase sales by showcasing their products to shoppers on Google and other search engine sites. To enable this feature, go to your *Seller Dashboard*, click on the *Settings* tab, and select *Offsite Ads*.

As we discussed a few sections back, if you sell less than $10,000 in a year on Etsy, you can choose whether or not to participate in *Etsy Offsite Ads*. However, if you exceed $10,000 in annual sales, *Offsite Ads* become mandatory. Since you only pay for the ad when someone orders something from you, there is no risk to the program.

PRO TIP: Because I focus heavily on Etsy SEO, I don't run regular *Etsy Ads* as I can get organic traffic from customers using the site. However, I do make sure I have opted into the *Offsite Ads* program. Again, I only pay for an offsite advertisement when it leads to a sale. To me, *Offsite Ads* are essentially free advertising for me as they bring people to my shop. If they make a purchase, I am then charged a small fee, which is easily covered by the money I made with the sale. Running my own Google Ads would cost a fortune, so the *Etsy Offsite Ads* program is a great benefit for me.

Payment Processing: When I started selling online in 2005 on eBay, getting paid was sometimes quite an adventure, to say the least. Back then, PayPal was the primary payment system used by eBay, and some customers were hesitant to trust the site. I had customers mail me checks and sometimes even cash through the mail to pay for their orders!

Fortunately, payment processing is now integrated into all online selling platforms, including Etsy. Thanks to *Etsy Payments*, I don't have to worry about collecting payments from my customers. Buyers can pay for their orders using different methods, such as credit and debit cards, PayPal, and gift cards. Etsy handles the payment processing, holding the funds in escrow until the seller confirms the shipment of the order.

This means that there's no need for sellers to send invoices or chase down payments, as everything is automated through Etsy.

Sales Tax: Selling on Etsy comes with a key advantage of the platform handling state sales tax collection and remittance on behalf of its sellers. This saves sellers a significant amount of time and effort as we don't have to collect and remit sales tax individually to each state, a requirement in most American states for online orders. This benefit of selling on Etsy is a major factor in why many sellers opt to keep their shop on the platform instead of setting up their own Shopify store. In fact, I have met successful Etsy shop owners who expanded to Shopify only to eventually go back to selling exclusively on Etsy for the sales tax collection alone!

Seller Protection: Etsy provides several protections for sellers on its platform, including:

Payment Protection: With Etsy Payments, buyers' funds are securely held until the order has been completed and the package has been delivered. This is why it is so important to ship your orders through Etsy so that tracking will automatically upload. When you buy and print your shipping labels on Etsy, both you and your customer will be given the package's unique tracking number. If the package is lost, you can file a claim through Etsy to refund the buyer and be reimbursed for your costs.

Dispute Resolution: Etsy's dispute resolution process is designed to help sellers and buyers resolve issues in a fair and timely manner. The process can involve either mediation, where Etsy acts as a mediator to facilitate communication between the parties, or arbitration, where Etsy makes a final decision on the dispute.

Both sellers and buyers can get help resolving any disputes through **Etsy's Help section.** Simply **scroll down to the bottom of any Etsy page** and locate the **Help** heading. Underneath, click on **Help Center.**

When possible, do your best to resolve customer issues on your own. When you are handmaking products, sometimes mistakes happen, especially when creating custom orders. If you made a mistake, make it right and issue the buyer a refund.

However, if a customer simply has buyer's remorse, be kind but firm in your response. Making sure you have a strict "no returns or exchanges" policy is vital to protect yourself from unwarranted return requests.

Seller Protection Insurance: Etsy's seller protection insurance is a program that provides coverage for eligible Etsy sellers who sell handmade products or craft supplies in their Etsy shops. Here's how it works:

When you sell a product on Etsy, you're automatically enrolled in Etsy's seller protection program. If a buyer files a case against you for an item that was not as described, or if the item was damaged or lost during shipping, you may be eligible for reimbursement or protection through the program.

To be eligible for seller protection, you must meet certain requirements, such as providing accurate descriptions and photos of your products, shipping orders promptly, and resolving any issues with buyers promptly.

If you're eligible for seller protection, Etsy may reimburse you for the cost of the item, shipping, and other associated costs, up to a maximum amount. The amount of coverage and the specific terms of the program may vary depending on the circumstances of the case.

It's important to note that seller protection is not a guarantee and may not cover all cases or circumstances. It's also important to take steps to protect yourself as a seller, such as using tracking and delivery confirmation, purchasing insurance for high-value items, and providing excellent customer service. If you want Etsy to have your back, you need to make sure you can prove that you did everything right on your end.

PRO TIP: If a buyer contacts you claiming an item hasn't been delivered but tracking shows it has, direct them to file a claim directly through Etsy. They can do this by clicking directly on their order and following the prompts on the screen. This removes you from the dispute process and puts the burden on Etsy directly to resolve the issue.

Shop Sections: Shop Sections, also referred to as your store categories, allow you to group your products into easy-to-navigate categories. This makes it simple for customers to find what they're looking for and for you to manage your inventory and listings more effectively.

To set up your Shop Sections, go to your **Seller Dashboard** and click on the **Listings** tab. On the right-hand side of the page will be the heading **Sections** with a drop-down menu underneath. Click on **Manage** to add and rearrange your shop categories. I personally like to arrange mine in alphabetical order.

Creating sections based on your different categories, niches, or special occasions and holidays will help customers easily narrow down the search results in your store. For example, if you sell personalized Christmas ornaments, you could create sections for each different recipient such as *Ornaments for Mom, Ornaments for Dad, Ornaments for Teachers*, etc.

PRO TIP: Remember that Etsy's search engine optimization (SEO) is a key aspect of selling on the platform. When you create a listing, it's important to use relevant keywords in the title, description, tags, and shop sections to help your item appear in search results.

For example, let's say you have created Christmas ornaments for children to give to their moms. When creating a listing for one of these ornaments, make sure to use "ornaments for mom" in the title, description, and tags. You can also create a shop section specifically for "ornaments for mom" to further improve your SEO. By using relevant keywords and categories, you're telling Etsy's search engine that your listing is relevant to someone searching for "ornaments for mom." This can increase the visibility of your listing and improve your chances of making a sale.

CHAPTER FOUR: LISTING YOUR CRAFTS ON ETSY

Now that you have set up your Etsy account and shop, it's time to start listing your crafts for sale! If you're new to selling online, it's normal to feel a bit nervous as you set out to create your first listing. But don't worry, in this chapter, I'll guide you step-by-step through the entire process. As you gain more experience, creating new listings will become easier and faster. These days I can create an Etsy listing in under a minute with one eye closed!

Before we dive into creating your first listing, I want to emphasize the importance of Etsy Search Engine Optimization (SEO) once again. I know, I know; you are probably sick of me talking about it. However, I cannot stress to you enough that the success of your Etsy shop is dependent on maximizing SEO. And just like creating new listings becomes easier with time, so does SEO.

To reiterate, SEO involves repeating important keywords in your listing title, description, tags, and shop sections. Unlike other e-commerce platforms where you only need to focus on loading keywords into listing titles, on Etsy it's essential to repeat keywords as much as possible. By repeating the most important keywords, you signal to Etsy that those are the terms they should prioritize when displaying your listings to customers.

Figuring out the most important keywords for each of your listings can be done with the help of keyword research tools such as EtsyCheck.com or eRank.com. As an example, let's say you make and sell candles. If you type *homemade candles* into EtsyCheck.com, you will be presented with a list of keywords ranked from the most searched to the least, including:

- Handmade candle
- Handmade candles
- Homemade candle
- Homemade candles
- Gift for her
- Cute candles
- Candle
- Candles
- Soy wax candle
- Scented candle
- Candle shop
- Home décor
- Birthday gift

This test search showed me that *Homemade candles* is a more popular keyword than *Handmade candles*. *Handmade* is used by shoppers looking for candle-making supplies, while *Homemade* is used by customers buying ready-made candles. If I were writing a title for a vanilla-scented handmade candle, it might be something like *Handmade Vanilla Scented Candle, Hand Poured Candles, Birthday Gift for Her, Cute Candle.*

I would then make sure to repeat these keywords in the listing description. *An example would be: Indulge in the sweet and soothing aroma of our handmade vanilla scented candle. Each candle is lovingly hand-poured using only the finest natural soy wax and pure vanilla essential oil, ensuring a long-lasting and delightful fragrance that will fill your home with warmth and comfort. Perfect for any occasion, this candle makes a wonderful birthday gift for her or a lovely addition to your own home decor. With its cute and charming design, it's sure to add a touch of cozy elegance to any room. Our candles are made in small batches to ensure the highest quality, and each one is carefully crafted with attention to detail. We use only eco-friendly materials and natural wicks, so you can enjoy a clean and sustainable burning experience. This vanilla scented candle has a burn time of approximately 35-40 hours, making it the perfect choice for a relaxing evening at home or a romantic dinner for two. Order now and experience the warm and inviting aroma of our handmade vanilla scented candle for yourself.*

I would then add the most important keywords into the *Tags* section of the listing, perhaps using the following:

1. Handmade candles
2. Vanilla candles
3. Scented candles
4. Natural soy wax
5. Home decor
6. Aromatherapy
7. Relaxation
8. Birthday gift for her
9. Eco-friendly
10. Long burn time
11. Hand poured
12. Essential oils
13. Cute candles

To maximize your chances of getting discovered by potential customers, it's important to organize your listings into appropriate shop sections. For instance, using the candle example, you could create a dedicated section for *Vanilla Candles* and add your vanilla scented candles to this category. By doing this, your candle will be easier for customers to find and purchase.

Since you've already repeated the term "vanilla candles" three times in your listing and in a shop section, Etsy's algorithm will likely pick up on this keyword and show your listing to customers who search for "vanilla candle." Additionally, Etsy will prioritize your vanilla candle when displaying ads on Google and social media platforms, further increasing your visibility to potential customers.

While you can repeat keywords in your titles, descriptions, and tags, you only get one shop section per item. Therefore, you want the shop section you add each item in to have the most relevant keyword. Using our candle example, "Vanilla Candles" is the most important keyword. Therefore, it makes for a good shop section.

Repeating keywords in your Etsy listings may feel tedious, but it's a necessary part of selling on the platform. You're competing with thousands of other sellers who offer products similar to yours, so simply listing an item and hoping it will be found isn't enough. By using SEO techniques, you can ensure that your products appear in relevant search results. And after a while, it becomes easier and easier to figure out the best keywords on your own without having to do any research.

Now that the SEO lecture is (once again!), out of the way, let's get to listing!

To create your first Etsy listing, log into your **Etsy Shop Manager**. Remember that your *Shop Manager* tab is easily located at the top of all your Etsy account pages; it's the little **shop icon**. After clicking on your *Shop Manager*, then click on the **Listings tab** on the left-hand side of the page. Then click on the **+ Add a listing** tab in the top right-hand corner of the page. This will bring up a blank listing template with the following fields to fill out:

Title: The Title section is one of the most important parts of your Etsy listing. It's the first thing customers will see when they're browsing through search results, so it needs to be descriptive and eye-catching. Etsy allows 140 characters in each title, and I recommend you use as many characters as possible to give your listing the best chance possible to be found in search results.

Good titles use descriptive words that accurately describe the item and use the most important keywords that customers might search for. Be sure to highlight any special features your item has. Avoid using all caps except for one or two of the most important words. Typing in all caps is considered "yelling" on the internet, so titles written in all caps have an off-putting effect on shoppers.

As an example of a good title, let's say you sell custom jewelry and are listing a necklace specifically for moms. A good title would be *Handmade Mom Necklace, Personalized Mother's Day Gift, Christmas Birthday Gift for Mom, Custom Jewelry, Personalized Gifts for Women.*

You want to make sure the keywords you use in your titles are the ones customers are searching for. This is why a research tool such as EtsyCheck or eRank comes in handy. You just enter a few words about the item you are listing, and they will find the keywords that Etsy shoppers are using to find products like yours.

Photos: Adding at least one photo to your Etsy listing is mandatory. However, Etsy allows you to upload up to 10 photos per listing. Try to use all 10 slots if possible, as this gives potential customers a better sense of what your product looks like from different angles and perspectives. A good tip is to make sure your photos give the customer the same views as if they were holding the item in their own hands and turning it over to examine all sides.

The first photo in your listing, called the *thumbnail* photo, is the most important picture as it's the one that customers will see in search results and on the listing page. *Thumbnail* photos should measure 2000x2000 pixels.

Providing clear, well-lit, and visually appealing photos is key. You don't need to have a professional photography set up; most sellers, including myself, take listing photos with an iPhone. Here are some tips for taking good Etsy listing photos:

1. **Use natural lighting:** Photograph your item in natural light, preferably near a window or outdoors. Add in lighting from lamps or ring lights as needed.
2. **Use a plain background:** Choose a clean, simple background that won't distract from your item. A white or neutral-colored backdrop works well. I use white foam boards that I buy at dollar stores.
3. **Get up close:** Take photos that show your item up close, so that potential customers can see the details and quality of your work.
4. **Use a tripod:** Use a tripod or steady surface to keep your camera steady and avoid blurry photos. Alternatively, you can use your phone's self-timer or a remote shutter.
5. **Show your item in use:** Consider including lifestyle photos that show your item in use or in a setting, as this can help potential customers envision how they might use or wear it.
6. **Take multiple photos:** Take multiple photos from different angles and perspectives to give potential customers a better sense of what your item looks like.
7. **Edit your photos:** Use basic photo editing tools to adjust the brightness, contrast, and color balance of your photos. Crop areas to zoom in on special details.

To get inspiration for styling your listing photos, take a look at how other sellers are photographing similar items in your niche. The goal isn't to copy but to get a better idea of the types of photos that are resonating with customers. Pay attention to lighting, backgrounds, and composition, and think about how you can apply these techniques to your photos.

If you're struggling to take high-quality photos, consider hiring a local photographer to take professional shots of your products. A photographer who's just starting their business may be more affordable than someone who's been in the industry for years. You could even consider bartering for their services by offering free products in exchange for photography and advertising their business along with your products. By investing in professional photos, especially if you sell more expensive items, you can give your listings a competitive edge and attract more potential customers.

Video: Etsy also allows you to include a video in your listing, which can help showcase your product in action and give customers a better idea of how it works. This can be especially useful if your product has unique features or requires some explanation. You can upload a video from your computer or embed one from YouTube or Vimeo. Adding videos to your Etsy listings is optional, but if you have the time and skill to do so, a video can help make your product stand out from the competition. Because videos are limited to no longer than 15 seconds and don't include sound, a short clip taken from your smart phone is all you need.

You can even consider using the same photo in multiple listings. For example, if you sell bath bombs, consider creating one video where you show multiple versions together. The idea is to show the customer the size and overall look of your products, not necessarily create a separate video for every single bath bomb you sell.

Description: The *Description* section in an Etsy listing is where you provide more detailed information about your product and expand upon what you included in the title. The first few lines of your description should give potential customers a brief overview of your product. Use this space to highlight its key features and benefits, and to make it clear who your product is intended for.

Next, be sure to include a list of the materials you used to create your product, as well as its dimensions or size. This information can help potential customers understand the quality and craftsmanship of your product. Even if you sell items that you don't think customers want the measurements for, include them anyway. You will be surprised by how many questions you get about measurements if you don't include them in the listing.

If your product is customizable, make sure to include instructions on how customers can personalize their orders. There is a separate area within each Etsy listing for sellers to explain what information they need from buyers to create custom orders, but you still want to include the instructions in the *Description*.

Note that online shoppers, including those on Etsy, are notorious for not reading listing descriptions and simply buying based on the photo. Making sure you include all of the details in your listing will protect you from cases where buyers claim their order didn't exactly match the photo or that the size wasn't what they expected.

If your product makes a good gift, be sure to mention this in your description. Include details on gift wrapping options, if you want to offer any, or any special touches you can add to make your product an even more thoughtful gift. I mentioned earlier in this book that offering gift wrapping can lead to more work for you as a seller, but offering to include a handwritten or typewritten gift card may be easier for you to manage.

Finally, even though your shipping and return policies will be shown in a dedicated section of your listing, it's a good idea to include them in your listing descriptions. Again, the more places you can include details and policies, the better, as it will protect you from complaints after the sale.

Here's an example of what a description might look like for the sample product referenced earlier that we titled *Handmade Mom Necklace, Personalized Mother's Day Gift, Christmas Birthday Gift for Mom, Custom Jewelry, Personalized Gifts for Women:*

This handmade Mom Necklace makes a thoughtful and personalized gift for Mother's Day, Christmas, birthdays, or any special occasion. The necklace is made from high-quality materials, including a sterling silver chain and a customizable birthstone pendant. You can personalize the necklace with the name of your choice for a truly one-of-a-kind gift. Each necklace is handcrafted with care and attention to detail and is sure to become a cherished keepsake for the special woman in your life. Shipping is available within five business days and gift wrapping is available upon request. Note that all customer jewelry orders are final; no returns or exchanges. Order now to create a custom jewelry piece that will be treasured for years to come!

Personalization: The personalization section of an Etsy listing allows you as a seller to provide custom options or personalization for your customers. This can be anything from adding a name or a specific date to a product to choosing a particular color or design.

If you will not be offering personalization, simply remove the option. Note that you can also make personalization optional.

PRO TIP: If you plan to offer both personalization and non-personalization, I recommend creating two separate listings for your product. Because you will likely want to charge more to customize products, you will want that option to be separate as it will be less confusing for the customers who see your lowest price but are confused about paying more for personalization. For example, if you sell baby onesies that come as-is or with the upcharge of embroidering the name onto the outfit, I would list both options separately so as not to confuse customers.

If you are going to offer personalization, the first thing you will need to decide is what type of personalization you will offer for your products. Will it be something simple like adding a name or date, or something more complex like custom colors or designs?

Once you have decided on the type of personalization, create a template that outlines the information you will need from your customers to complete the personalization. For example, if you are offering a custom name option, you will need to know the name that the customer wants to have added.

Etsy provides a section for buyers to tell you their customization options. You can choose a character limit for this section, anywhere from 1 to 1024. I would choose 1024 to give your buyers maximum space for communicating with you.

It is also important that you make sure that you can fulfill the personalization requests promptly. If you have a high volume of orders, you will want to change your handling time. This usually happens around the holidays when people are shopping for gifts, so think ahead to the busy season when you will need more time to handle custom orders.

Price: It's now time to price your item! If you have been selling your crafts locally, you may need to make some adjustments to pricing them on Etsy. In many instances, you will likely be able to charge more for your handmade items on Etsy than you can in your area. Be sure to look at what other Etsy shops that sell products similar to yours are charging to get an idea of where to start.

Using an Etsy fee calculator is a great way to figure out how much profit you will make per sale. I use omniprofitcalculator.com/etsy-fee-calculator.

As an example, let's say you make soy candles that you normally charge $10 for at craft show. Using an Etsy fee calculator, you would enter your item price as $10. Because Etsy utilizes calculated shipping where they figure out the postage costs for you based on the weight of the package and zip codes it is shipping from and to, we'll just use $5 as our shipping charge and shipping cost for this example. You spent $4 in supplies to create your candle and use Etsy's Direct Checkout payment processing to complete orders. After Etsy fees, your net profit for the $10 candle would be $4.12.

Calculating your net profit on Etsy requires factoring in all expenses associated with running your business. While a profit margin of $4.12 may seem nice, it's important to remember that this amount does not cover all of your expenses. In addition to reinvesting some of your profits into your business, you will also need to allocate funds for office supplies, internet service, shipping supplies, and taxes on any earnings.

When you consider all of these expenses, suddenly your $4.12 profit margin looks a lot less substantial. However, by increasing the price you charge customers to $15, your profit after fees and shipping increases to $8.65 - a significant improvement over the original profit margin of $4.12. This illustrates the importance of carefully considering your pricing strategy and factoring in all expenses when calculating your net profit on Etsy.

Consider this pricing trick: Raise the price of your item to $20 and offer "free" shipping for your candles. Keep in mind that "free" shipping isn't actually free, as you will have to cover the shipping costs by including them in the item price. However, by doing this, your listing will show up as "free shipping" on Etsy, which can improve your item's ranking in search results.

It's important to note that "free" shipping may not always be feasible, especially if you're selling custom products or large, bulky items. However, for smaller, less fragile items like jewelry and clothing that can ship for under one pound, offering "free" shipping may give you a competitive edge in the marketplace. By implementing this pricing strategy, you can potentially attract more customers and increase your sales on Etsy.

Etsy also pushes for sellers to opt into their "free shipping on orders of $35 or more" setting. If you sell lower-dollar items, opting into this program may lead to higher order totals as customers add more to their shopping carts to hit the $35 threshold.

PRO TIP: Even if you offer free shipping on all of your products, still opt into Etsy's $35 free shipping promotion as they will add your shop to the program.

Most sellers experiment with different prices to see what works best for their products. Etsy allows you to change your prices at any time, so you can adjust your prices based on customer feedback or changes in your costs.

Quantity: The *Quantity* section of an Etsy listing allows you to specify how many of a particular item you have available for sale. Here are some tips for filling out this section:

1. **Determine your inventory:** Before listing your item, you should determine how many of the items you have available for sale. This can be based on how many items you have already made or how many you can realistically produce within a certain time frame.

2. **Enter the quantity:** Once you have determined your inventory, enter the number of items that you have available for sale in the "Quantity" section of your listing.

3. **Consider variations:** If you offer different variations of your item (such as different colors or sizes), you will need to enter the quantity for each variation separately. I prefer creating separate listings for different variations, but that is a personal choice.

4. **Update as needed:** If you sell an item and your inventory decreases, be sure to update the quantity in your listing. This will help to avoid overselling and ensure that you can fulfill all of your orders.

5. **Limit the quantity:** If you have a limited quantity of an item (such as a one-of-a-kind item), you may want to consider limiting the quantity available for sale to create a sense of exclusivity and urgency for customers.

Core Details/Production Partners: Etsy often makes slight changes to their listing forms; and sometimes your layout depends on your location. As of this writing, some people might see "Core Details", while others will see "Production Partners". No matter what it is called both sections cover the same thing and that is for you to disclose if you are using a third-party manufacturer or producer to create your items.

As we've already discussed, if you are making your crafts using craft supplies, you do not have to disclose those sources. You only have to disclose if you have outsourced any of the work needed to make your product. Etsy has specific guidelines for using production partners, so be sure to review these before filling out this section. In general, you must disclose if you are using a production partner and provide accurate information about their role in creating your items.

However, even if you aren't using a Production Partner, you will still have to answer the following:

Who made it?

- I did (a product you made completely yourself with the use of craft supplies)
- A member of my shop (an employee in your shop)
- Another company or person (any Production Partners you used)

What is it?

- A finished product (a ready-to-use item, even if it needs to be customized)
- A supply or tool to make things (craft supplies or equipment)

When was it made?

- Made to order (best for crafts, even if you have products already made and ready to ship)
- The year it was made

If you are using a third-party to help create your items, enter their name or names in the *Production Partners* section of your listing. You can choose to private the name of the company, but customers will get a notice that you had assistance creating your item. information will be visible to customers. If your production partner changes or you stop using one, be sure to update the *Production Partners* section of your listing to reflect these changes. Remember that you don't have to disclose where you purchased the supplies to create your items as craft supplies and stores aren't production partners.

Category: The *Category* section of an Etsy listing allows you to select the most relevant category for your item, which in turn will help shoppers find you. Etsy will usually offer you suggestions based on your title, but you can override those options by typing in your product into the search bar to see what comes up.

Before selecting a category, consider what category your product fits into best. For example, if you sell handmade jewelry, you will want to select the "Jewelry" category. But if you have an item that doesn't seem to fit in a specific category, try searching for similar items on Etsy's site to see what categories similar products are in.

Most categories on Etsy have subcategories. The great thing about this is that Etsy will automatically put your listing in both the main category and any relevant subcategories, which increases the chance of your item being found in the search. Select as many subcategories as Etsy offers you to widen your net on the site.

Tags: The *Tags* section of an Etsy listing is where you can add relevant keywords that describe your item. Tags help customers to find your item when they search for those specific keywords on Etsy. As previously mentioned, *Tags* are a part of Etsy SEO. You want to repeat relevant keywords in your *Title, Description, Shop Section,* and *Tags* to give them the best chance of being found in search.

As I've already mentioned, I use both eRank and EtsyCheck to search for the best *Tags* for my listings. Sites such as these give me the keywords that Etsy shoppers are typing into search and also show me which keywords lead to sales.

Etsy allows you to add up to 13 *Tags* for each item. Be sure to use all of the available tags to maximize your book's visibility in search results. I like to use a mix of the most popular keywords along with some that are lower in rank to spread my reach as wide as possible. Because

Etsy is such a competitive marketplace, using a handful of less relevant keywords can help reach more customers.

PRO TIP: You can bulk edit *Tags* in your *Shop Manager.* Simply click on the *Listings* tab and click the box next to the listings to which you want to add *Tags* to. Then select *Editing Options* and choose *Edit tags* from the drop-down menu.

The bulk edit feature is helpful if you are listing very similar items back-to-back. For example, if you are listing Christmas ornaments for grandmothers, the *Tags* will likely all be the same for each listing. You can type up your *Tags* in a Word document and, using the bulk edit feature, copy and paste *Tags* into several listings at once. Note that you can also use the bulk edit feature for several fields within your listings

Materials: While some Etsy categories have a listing section where you can choose materials from a drop-down menu, the options in these menus can be limited. Fortunately, there is another section in the listing template where you can manually add the materials you use in making your crafts. This section is located under the *Tags* field and allows you to add as many relevant materials as you need.

This manual tagging process is particularly helpful for crafters who use materials that are not listed in the drop-down menus. For example, if you make jewelry using unusual gemstones or beads, the manual tagging process allows you to add those specific materials to your listing so that customers can find your items when they search for those specific materials.

The manual tagging section allows sellers to provide more detailed information about the materials they use. Another example would be if you make soap and use natural, organic ingredients. You can use the *Materials* field to enter those exact details to target customers looking for those specific materials.

Shipping: Well, we've reached the section of the listing that most new online sellers fear. Shipping. I devote an enter chapter to shipping on Etsy later in the next chapter of this book. But for now, here's a quick step-by-step instruction list:

1. To accurately calculate shipping costs, you will need a digital postage scale to weight packages for shipment. These can be found for under $20 on Amazon.
2. Weigh the item you are listing inside of a shipping box. It doesn't have to be the box you end up using to ship the product, but you want a similar size box to get an estimated weight. You also want to add a few ounces to account for the weight of packing materials.
3. If the package weighs less than one pound, you can ship it via USPS First Class. This is the most cost-effective option for lightweight packages.
4. If the package weighs over one pound, you will need to ship it via USPS Parcel or Priority. Parcel is generally the most cost-effective option for heavier packages, but Priority may be faster, cost the same or even less than Parcel, and provides additional shipping options such as insurance.
5. Enter the package weight when listing the item on Etsy. This will allow Etsy to present you with the available shipping options.
6. Select the shipping option(s) you want to offer customers. Consider offering multiple shipping options to accommodate customers with different needs and budgets.
7. When a customer places an order, Etsy will calculate the postage based on the weight you entered and the shipping option they selected. The cost will also depend on the distance between you and your customer. If you are in Florida and shipping to a customer in Florida, the cost will be less

than if you are shipping to a customer in California.

8. Once Etsy has determined the cost, you can purchase and print the shipping label through Etsy. The cost of the label will be deducted from your balance. Be sure to double-check the shipping address and package weight before purchasing the label.

9. Because you printed the label through Etsy, both you and the customer will be given the tracking information. This allows you and the customer to track the package during shipping and ensures that the package arrives safely.

10. You can also print out a packing ship during this process.

Returns & Exchanges: Most sellers of handmade goods do not allow for returns or exchanges unless they made a mistake in producing the product. However, this is only a decision you can make. Note that if you made a mistake, it's easier to issue the customer a full refund and allow them to keep the product rather than ask them to ship the product back to you and pay for the return shipping.

Shop Section: As we've already discussed, *Shop Sections* are your Etsy store categories. Remember that you want to make sure your listing titles match your shop sections to maximize Etsy SEO. You can have 20 sections in your shop, and you can edit them at any time.

Renewal Options: When you list an item for sale on Etsy, you have the option to choose between *Manual Renewal* and *Automatic Renewal. Manual Renewal* means that after four months, Etsy will end your listing. You will then need to manually renew it. With *Automatic Renewal,* Etsy will automatically renew the listing every four months.

I always recommend that when you first list an item you choose *Manual Renewal* as it allows you to reevaluate the listing after four months and make any necessary edits or adjustments. This allows you to see how your listing is performing and make changes to improve it.

However, if after four months, you see that a listing has been selling well, I recommend that you relist it but change the setting to *Automatic Renewal.* You will then not have to manually renew it every four months, which will ensure that your listing stays active and continues to attract new buyers.

Publish: Once you have filled out the listing form and have doubled checked to make sure everything is correct, you simply click on the *Publish* button, which will make the listing live on Etsy's site. Your item is now available for sale on Etsy!

Listing Your Second Item: Once you have published your first listing, it's time to tackle the second. However, instead of starting from scratch by clicking on the + *Add a listing* button, you can use the "sell similar" method of simply making a *Copy* of an existing listing and changing the item specifics. It works particularly well if you are listing similar items back-to-back. The Copy option is found on the photo of each listing; just **click on the little screw icon** to bring it up.

For example, a jewelry seller could use the "sell similar" method to list several necklaces one after the other. They could start by duplicating the listing for one of their necklaces, and then make changes to the item specifics, such as the color, size, or materials used, to create a new listing for a different necklace.

Just Keep Listing: Note that it takes awhile to build a successful Etsy shop. It's hard to get people to buy from you when you only have a few items listed. The fact is that the most successful Etsy shops have hundreds and sometimes thousands of active listings. Remember my tip about listing variations separately. For example, if you sell pottery, list every size and color separately to maximize your listings. Set a goal to list at least five items every day. It may take awhile for customers to find your shop, but in the meantime, just keep listing!

CHAPTER FIVE: ETSY SHIPPING MADE EASY

The time has come: You've made your first Etsy sale! You can enable notifications on your smartphone through the Etsy app so that you will get a message every time an order comes in. Or you need to make a point to check your *Seller Dashboard* at least twice daily to see if you have any new orders. But regardless of how you check your account, there is an order awaiting shipment!

FUN FACT: If you enable notifications, you will hear a cash register sound every time you make a sale! There's nothing better than hearing that CHA-CHING sound as it means you are making money!

However, once a sale has come through, a new job starts as you will need to ship out the order. But before you can package an order, you need shipping supplies. Because crafts come in all shapes and sizes, what shipping supplies you need will vary based on what you sell. If you sell jewelry, you may want to invest in cardboard jewelry boxes with cushioned inserts (you can buy these in bulk on Amazon). If you sell cards, you may want to purchase cardboard mailers to ensure orders aren't bent during the shipping process. And if you are shipping larger items, you will need shipping boxes.

But boxes are just the start of the shipping supplies you will need to sell your crafts on Etsy. Here is what most Etsy sellers keep on hand for their businesses:

Digital Postage Scale: The number one supply you MUST have if you are going to sell your crafts on Etsy is a digital postal scale to weigh packages to figure out the correct postage. You can buy digital scales for around $20 to $30 on Amazon, and they are also sold at office supply stores. Look for a "postage/mail" specific scale that measures pounds AND ounces, as you will need to know ounces when shipping via USPS First Class mail.

Some sellers choose to charge a flat rate for all their orders. These sellers tend to sell the same types of items, such as jewelry or cards. For example, many jewelry sellers charge $5 to ship any of their items as everything they sell weighs under one pound and ships via First Class.

If you sell items that weigh over one pound, you will want to let Etsy calculate the shipping cost for both you and your customer based on the weight of the package and the distance between your two zip codes. This method ensures that the customer pays the exact postage needed for you to ship them their order.

Note that some sellers offer *free shipping*, padding the item's cost into their estimated shipping charge. While offering free shipping is a smart move for lightweight items that weigh under one pound, it can backfire on heavier items as buyers know when a seller has inflated the price of an item to cover shipping. For example, if you sell handmade woven baskets, it will be hard to add the $10 to $20 shipping cost to the price of your baskets.

Printer & Labels: There are a few different options for addressing and posting your Etsy orders. The first is to simply print labels onto paper, cut them out, and tape them to boxes. People laugh when I tell them I used this method for many years! But it was cost-effective and worked. You can certainly start by using this method, especially if you are completely new to shipping and just want to get used to the process.

These days, using a shipping label printer is arguably the most efficient and professional way to print shipping labels. On Etsy, you can purchase and print shipping labels directly from the platform. This will save you time and effort compared to handwriting addresses or taking orders to the post office.

To print shipping labels from Etsy, you'll need a printer that is compatible with the labels you are using. There are two different types of printers that you can use:

Thermal Printer: This type of printer doesn't use ink, but it does require special labels. It's a good option if you want to avoid the hassle of replacing ink cartridges or toner. A thermal printer works by using heat to transfer inkless media onto paper. It consists of a print head with a row of tiny heating elements that are activated according to the digital image of the document being printed. When the heating elements are activated, they cause a thermal reaction in the inkless media, which results in the transfer of the media onto the paper.

I use a Rollo thermal printer specifically for printing my Etsy sticker shop order labels. While I do not have to purchase ink for the printer, I do have to buy special labels.

LaserJet Printer: This type of printer uses toner to print, and it can be a good option for printing shipping labels as well as packing slips for larger orders. LaserJet printers are known for their speed, reliability, and high-quality printing as well as their affordable pricing. They can print on a wide range of media, including envelopes, labels, and cardstock.

LaserJet printers are more efficient and cost-effective than inkjet printers when it comes to printing large volumes of documents. However, they do require toner, which can be more expensive than ink in the long run. I use a thermal printer to print shipping labels but use my LaserJet printer to print packing slips for larger Etsy orders.

Freebies: Including free items in orders is a common practice among Etsy shops. This can be a nice way to show appreciation to your customers and promote your business. Stickers or magnets with your URL or brand name are the most popular freebies as they offer an affordable way for you to promote your business and encourage customers to visit your shop or website. I use StickerMule to print my enclosure stickers. I have a wide variety of both stickers and magnets with my URL printed on them.

Some sellers include freebies that coordinate with the shop offerings. For example, if a shop sells candles, they may include a book of matches in each order. If they sell jewelry, the pieces might come is a small jewelry bag with their shop's logo printed on it. You can purchase these types of freebies from sites such as Oriental Trading Company, Alibaba, Temu, and Amazon.

Boxes & Envelopes: You cannot just stick a shipping label directly onto your handmade item and stick it in the mail box. Shipping packages require *shipping supplies*, and that means shipping boxes and envelopes, such as:

- **Plain cardboard shipping boxes in various sizes**
- **USPS Priority shipping boxes**
- **Poly mailers**
- **Bubble mailers**
- **Cardboard envelope mailers**

The United States Postal Service (USPS) is a great resource for small businesses because they offer FREE *Priority Mail* shipping boxes. While *Priority Mail* is an excellent option for shipping many packages, you will need other forms of packaging if you sell items that qualify for *Media Mail, First Class Mail,* and *Parcel Select,* as well as for international shipments (again, more on these forms of shipping coming up). Basically, you need two forms of shipping boxes/ envelopes: *Priority Mail* boxes and envelopes, and plain boxes and envelopes for the rest.

USPS Standard Priority Boxes: The sizes of boxes you will need depends on what you sell. You can order Priority Boxes for free online; your mail carrier will deliver them to your door. Here are the most popular box sizes:

- **Priority Mail Show Box SHOEBOX:** 14-7/8 x 7-3/8 x 5.24 (not just for shoes, but for anything long and narrow)
- **Priority Mail Box 1097 Rectangle:** 11-5/8 x 2.5x 13-7/16
- **Priority Mail Box 1905 Rectangle:** 12.5 x 3-1/8 x 15-5/8
- **Priority Mail Box 1092 Rectangle:** 12.25 x 2-7/8 x 13-11/16
- **Priority Mail Box 1096L Rectangle:** 9-7/16 x 6-7/16 x 2-3/16
- **Large Priority Mail Box 7:** 12.25 x 12 x 8.5 (largest size of the Priority Mail boxes; perfect for shipping larger products or several smaller items in one box)
- **Priority Mail Box 4:** 7.25 x 7.25 x 6.25 (square size is perfect for shipping mugs, figurines, and small, rounded items)

- **Priority Mail Padded Flat Rate Envelope:** 9.5 x 12.5 (the go-to choice for shipping heavy clothing, shoes, and anything that you can stuff into a package)

In addition to the FREE boxes, you can also order FREE **USPS Priority Stickers,** which are perfect for covering writing on the outside of repurposed boxes.

- **Priority Mail Sticker Label Roll of 1000**
- **Priority Mail Shipping Label of 10**

When you look through all the available choices for *Priority Mail* boxes and envelopes, you will see that USPS offers many other options that I did not list above, including Flat Rate and Express boxes. As you continue along your Etsy journey, you will learn which shipping boxes and envelopes you use the most, and therefore, which you need to reorder frequently. You'll also know if you want to branch out into Flat Rate or Express packaging.

The Post Office offers these free shipping supplies in quantities as low as ten each. Depending on the sizes of products you sell, you may want to order some of each just to have them on hand. However, I find that I mostly use Box 7, Box 4, and the Padded Flat Rate Envelopes the most, although I do keep a small supply of the rectangle boxes on hand as well as the "shoe box", which is great for longer items that are too thick to fit in the rectangle boxes.

Note that sometimes it can take quite a while for Priority boxes to be delivered due to supply issues, so do not wait until you are completely out to order more, especially heading into the busy holiday season. I order my supply of *Priority Mail* boxes in September in anticipation of the fourth quarter. While some Post Office locations keep a supply in stock, many do not. My location has to order boxes the same way I do to stock their retail section!

While *Priority Mail* is an excellent option for shipping most packages, you will need other forms of packaging for **Media Mail** (if you sell books), **First Class Mail** (for packages under 1 pound), and **Parcel Select** (for boxes too large to ship via Priority), as those methods of postage can NOT be mailed in the *Priority Mail* boxes. It is also against USPS policy to alter the *Priority* boxes in any way, so forget thinking you can turn them inside out (they are printed with *Priority Mail* on the inside to thwart this) or put stickers on the outside to conceal the fact that they are indeed *Priority*. Misusing USPS supplies can result in your losing your postal account.

Before you run out and buy new shipping boxes and envelopes, however, check around your house to see what you have on hand.

Plain cardboard boxes, manila envelopes, and bubble mailers can all be used for non-priority mail as long as they are in good, clean condition. While eBay sellers can get away with patching up beat-up boxes, Etsy sellers cannot. I save every strong, clean shipping box I receive as well as good packing materials.

Take an inventory of the various sizes of your crafts to determine the packaging you will need. Perhaps you will only sell textiles, for which poly and bubble mailers are enough. On the other hand, if you sell baskets, you do not need to worry about stocking up on envelopes.

I sell different types of products on several different platforms, so I keep a wide variety of boxes and envelopes in my shipping supply area. While I utilize the free *Priority Mail* boxes and bubble mailers from the Post Office, I invest in plain shipping boxes from Amazon, eBay, Uline, and Value Mailers for *Media, First Class,* and *Parcel* packages. I also have manila bubble mailer envelopes that I buy at Sam's Club and poly mailers that I order on Amazon. I keep the following plain boxes and envelopes on hand:

- **Plain Cardboard Shipping Boxes** (4", 6", 8", 10", and 12" sizes)
- **Oversized Cardboard Shipping Boxes** (14" and 16" sizes for when I have to ship oversized items via Parcel or UPS)
- **Poly Mailers in various sizes** (for shipping clothing and plush)
- **Bubble Mailers in various sizes** (for items that need more cushioning than a plain poly mailer)
- **Cardboard Mailers in various sizes** (for shipping paper products that I do not want bending in the mail)

Packing Materials: You cannot just throw an item into a box and ship it with no packing materials to buffer it inside the box (well, you CAN, as I have seen many sellers do, but you should not). You need to WRAP up your items to protect them inside the box. You want to ensure that the item is protected from being thrown around, inside planes and trucks, and tossed onto customers' porches. Depending on what you sell and how much protection your products need, these are supplies you may want to consider:

- **Recycled Packing Paper** (to wrap up items inside of the shipping box)
- **Bubble Wrap** (essential for protecting breakables)
- **Packing Peanuts** (perfect for buffering breakables inside of boxes)
- **Shipping Tape** (buy the largest rolls and the strongest type you can)
- **Tissue Paper** (better than packing paper for wrapping delicate breakables)
- **Cardboard Corrugated Rolls** (allows you to create a box-in-a-box around breakables)

Shipping Tape: You now have an assortment of boxes, envelopes, packing paper, newspaper, bubble wrap, packing peanuts, cardboard rolls, and/or tissue paper to protect your items during shipping. To seal your packages, you need shipping tape.

Note that you want to purchase *SHIPPING tape,* not packing tap*e*. Packing tape is for moving boxes and is not as strong, while shipping tape is meant to hold packages together as they travel to their destination by vehicle, boat, and/or air.

Most sellers use a **handheld tape dispenser** (usually sold right next to the tape at stores). If you are just starting out selling on Etsy, I recommend buying a kit with the tape dispenser included with extra rolls of tape. You can usually find such kits for $10 to $15 in the tape section of the big box stores. You only need to buy the dispenser once and then just buy tape refills as needed. Throughout the year, the shipping tape at Sam's Club and Costco goes on sale; when it does, I stock up. These warehouse clubs offer the best deal on shipping tape. If you don't have a location near you, you can order from both online.

Now for the most confusing part of selling on Etsy for new sellers: **Shipping!**

There are dozens of carriers and ways you can ship packages. While UPS and FedEx are viable shipping options, you will want to stick with shipping your packages through the United States Postal Service (USPS) when you are just starting your online business. The USPS provides the best value and service for small sellers, and Etsy has partnered with them to make shipping easy and cost-effective. Since the USPS is Etsy's preferred shipping partner, if you sell on Etsy, you will be using them a lot.

While there are numerous ways you can ship a package through the Post Office, most Etsy sellers ship via one of four methods, all of which are for shipments within the United States (including San Juan, Puerto Rico, and military bases):

- **Media Mail**
- **First Class Mail**
- **Parcel Select**
- **Priority Mail**

Media Mail: Media Mail is for, surprise, MEDIA! It is preferable to ship books via *Media Mail* because they are heavy, and you get a discounted rate. However, the low price also means that *Media Mail* is extremely slow, sometimes taking up to one month (although the Post Office claims delivery is two to eight business days).

The following items qualify to be shipped via *Media Mail*:

- **Books of at least eight printed pages**
- **16-millimeter or narrower-width films and catalogs of films 24 pages or more**
- **Printed music**
- **Educational testing materials and printed educational materials**
- **Sound recordings**
- **Playscripts and manuscripts**
- **Loose-leaf pages and their binders of education medical information**
- **Computer-readable media**

Media Mail can NOT be used for advertising, video games, computer drives, or digital drives. The maximum weight for a *Media Mail* package is 70 pounds.

Some sellers try to cheat the system by shipping heavy, non-media items via *Media Mail*. This is a violation of the USPS policy and can result in you losing your postal account. Post offices are notorious for opening boxes marked as *Media Mail* to ensure they only contain approved media items, so be careful to follow the rules.

***Media Mail* items can only be shipped in plain boxes or envelopes**, NOT in *Priority Mail* boxes. When you print a label via Etsy (more on how to do this coming up), it will clearly state on the label which service you paid for. So, if you print a *Media Mail* label, it will say "MEDIA MAIL" at the top.

First Class: *First Class MAIL* is the service you use when you send a postcard or letter weighing 3.5 ounces or less. While one stamp equals one ounce on a rectangular postcard or letter up to 3.5 ounces, anything 4 ounces or larger is charged at a higher PACKAGE RATE.

Unless you are selling flat lightweight items that fit in letter envelopes, you will be paying the package rate to ship your Etsy orders.

You can ship up to 16 ounces (1-pound) via *First Class*. Like *Media Mail*, **First Class packages must be in plain boxes or envelopes;** you can NOT use the free *Priority Mail* boxes or envelopes to ship *First Class* packages.

Shipping items via *First Class* is where having a digital postage scale comes in handy, as you can get your package down to the exact ounce. The *First Class* cost varies by weight and zone, so it is essential to get as close a weight on your item as possible (I will talk more about weighing your packages coming up).

If you are using *Calculated Shipping* and having your customers pay the shipping charge, offering them *First Class* postage saves them money. For example, if the package you are sending weighs 8 ounces, the difference between *First Class* and *Parcel* or *Priority* can be as much as $6, depending on where the item is shipping to.

However, even with a digital scale, finding the exact ounce can be challenging as you need an item's weight before you list an item. My trick when dealing with items that will ship in poly mailers, and one that I will talk more about later in this book, is to add 3 ounces to the weight of these light packages to account for packing materials. So, if you have a small item that, on its own, weighs 5 ounces, list it as 8 ounces. That way, when it is in an envelope with bubble wrap or even just some tissue baby and a packing slip, you will not risk the Post Office sending it back for insufficient postage. Or worse, delivering it to your customer and them having to pay the difference!

Parcel Select: *Parcel Select*, formerly called *Parcel Post*, is for packages weighing over 16 ounces. *Parcel* is slower than *Priority* (shipping time can take up to two weeks, although the Post Office claims two to eight business days), but it is cheaper for heavy items. ***Parcel* shipments must be in plain boxes or envelopes**; just as with *Media Mail* and *First Class*, you can NOT ship *Parcel Select* shipments in the *Priority Mail* boxes. The maximum weight for *Parcel* packages is 70 pounds.

Parcel Select postage cost depends on the weight of the package and where it is going. That is why it is wise to use Etsy's *Calculated Shipping* as the customer pays for the exact shipping for their zip code.

While *Parcel Select* is an excellent option for heavy packages, you want to make sure to check the cost between *Parcel* and *Priority* when you are creating your shipping label through Etsy (again, I will be going over how to do this coming up). Depending on how far away the package is going, *Priority Mail* may be the cheaper option.

For example, I am in Iowa, centrally located on both coasts in the middle of the country. For packages weighing less than four pounds, it is often cheaper for me to ship via *Priority Mail* over *Parcel Select*. Plus, I get to use a free *Priority Mail* shipping box.

What is great about shipping through Etsy is you can look at all the package and price options before paying for and printing a label. That way, you can find the best rate AND fastest shipping time for each order. It is always nice when a customer pays for *Parcel,* but you can upgrade them to *Priority*. Not only do you save money by being able to use a free Priority box, but the item arrives much faster, which always makes customers happy.

Priority Mail: *Priority Mail* is for packages weighing over 16 ounces or more that need to get to their location quickly, typically in 2-3 business days. Note that "business days" means weekdays and does not include Saturdays, Sundays, or federal holidays. If you ship an item out on a Friday, realize that it may not be processed and scanned at your area

Post Office until Monday. From there, it will have an additional two to three days before it reaches the customer.

As I explained above when discussing *Parcel Select*, sometimes *Priority Mail* can be the cheaper option. For me, this is often true for packages weighing less than four pounds that go as far as the West or East coasts. In fact, most of my shipments go via *Priority Mail* as nine times out of ten, it ends up being the cheapest option for packages between one and four pounds and I save money as I can use a free Priority box.

Priority Mail has other bonuses over *Parcel Select,* including FREE tracking when you purchase the label online, Saturday delivery, and FREE **Carrier Pickup.** I utilize *Carrier Pickup* to have my mail carrier pick up my packages and scan them in immediately; however, I must have at least one *Priority Mail* or *First Class* package to request a pickup. For example, I cannot request this free pickup service if I have all *Parcel Select* packages. Since I work from home, *Carrier Pickup* is a blessing as I do not have to make multiple trips to the Post Office every week!

Of course, the best thing about *Priority Mail* is the FREE boxes! There are many sizes of *Priority Mail* boxes, some of which we've already discussed, including *Flat Rate* options. While the Post Office promotes their *Flat Rate* boxes as having the best postage costs, regular *Priority Mail* is usually cheaper for packages less than four pounds. Why? Because remember, when it comes to *Priority Mail,* it is not just the weight of the box but also the distance a package has to travel.

As I mentioned previously, I live in Iowa. I can send a two-pound package to Minnesota for a little over $7. However, that same package costs over $12 to ship to California. If that package goes to New York, the postage is around $11. To Hawaii or Alaska, the cost jumps to $15. Again, it is not just the weight but the distance the package must travel.

The type of *Priority Mail* box (*Regular or Flat Rate*) does not affect the speed of delivery. *Priority* is *Priority*. The difference in the shipping cost depends on the type and size of the box.

When packages are sorted for shipment at the Post Office, the most expensive postage options go first as they are guaranteed space on the trucks and planes. *Overnight* and *Express* are the most expensive since customers pay for one-to-two-day delivery. Next comes *Priority*, followed by *First Class*. *Media Mail* and *Bulk Mail* (bulk mail is usually "junk" mail that is sent out in mass) are the cheapest and, therefore, the last packages to be put out for delivery. It is all about available space; the more room on the truck or plane, the more packages they will ship out. is always in your best interest as a seller to use the fastest option available, even if you pay some change out of pocket. The faster the customer receives their order, the happier they will be!

The Post Office promotes *Priority Mail* as being delivered in two to three business days. Again, that is BUSINESS days, i.e., WEEKDAYS. While some large postal facilities process mail on the weekends, the vast majority do not. Mail and packages are not processed on federal holidays, either. Etsy stands behind sellers in shipping times when it comes to mailing out orders on weekends and holidays; keep these rules in mind if you have a customer demanding that the order they placed on Friday arrive by Monday. Etsy will also protect sellers in case of a major weather event or disaster for sellers in affected areas.

International Shipping: International shipping used to be such a massive headache that most sellers avoided it altogether. While you certainly do not need to ship to Canada, South America, or overseas, doing so will significantly increase your business. Fortunately, Etsy makes shipping international orders easy.

When you choose your domestic shipping options in a listing, you can also choose other countries you will ship orders to. Etsy will calculate the cost for the buyer, and the label you print will have the customs form information right on it. You simply put the label onto the package just as you would for a domestic order and the Post Office will handle the delivery.

One negative aspect of shipping internationally is that international packages' tracking varies greatly and is quite unreliable. While Canada, the United Kingdom, and Australia all offer easy-to-track, generally reliable shipments, there are some areas of the world you may want to consider avoiding. I have been selling online since 2005 and have shipped to every corner of the globe. That being said, these days I avoid shipping packages to Central and South America, Africa, the Middle East, and Italy.

While the other European countries offer fairly reliable shipping, Italy is notorious for holding packages up in customs and losing them. Mexico along with Central and South American counties also have poor tracking, and shipping anywhere in Africa or the Middle East is risky as many online scams originate from those regions. Most international customers who buy from American Etsy sellers are in Canada, England, and Australia; for many years, those were the only areas I would sell to.

Once a shipment arrives in the buyer's country, it must first go through customs. As I have mentioned, some countries do this very quickly, while others (Italy) are notoriously slow. International shipping can take as little as a week to arrive in Canada or up to a month or more for countries overseas. Fortunately, when you print shipping labels through Etsy, they protect lost or stolen packages.

How To Set Up Shipping In Your Listings: So now that you understand the basic four categories of USPS shipping options, it is time to choose the ones you want to offer for your listings. One of the biggest mistakes new Etsy sellers make is to guess shipping costs, resulting in either overcharging customers or undercharging them and losing money on shipping. However, **Calculated Shipping** will protect you and your customers from incorrect postage costs.

I firmly believe in using *Calculated Shipping* on Etsy for packages weighing over one pound. If you have a digital scale, there is no reason not to use *Calculated Shipping* as it means the buyer pays the exact shipping cost for the item's weight and the zip code it is being shipped to.

While more seasoned Etsy sellers like to experiment with "free" shipping (i.e., building the shipping cost into the price of an item), I recommend you stick to *Calculated Shipping* when you are just starting out selling and have the buyer pay shipping. This will protect you from LOSING money by trying to guess shipping costs. It also ensures a fair shipping rate for the customer, which will mean you will not get angry customers who figure they were overcharged for shipping. You can experiment with "free" shipping once you are more comfortable selling and shipping.

So, you have a digital postage scale and are ready to create a listing using *Calculated Shipping*. It is so easy to do; here is how:

First, put your item into a box similar to the one it will ship out in. Note that the box does not have to be the exact one you will end up shipping the item in; you just want a box close to the size and weight of the one you will be using. Boxes can easily add up to one pound of weight to a shipment, so you need to know what box you will use.

For example, if you are selling a set of handmade soaps, place them in a 7x7x6-inch Priority Mail box or a similar-sized box. Set the box on the digital scale and note the weight. Perhaps it comes out to one pound and four ounces.

Within the Etsy listing form, the shipping settings are located under **SHIPPING.**

Under **Shipping,** there is a box titled **Shipping option.** Click on **Select profile.** Then click **+ Create new profile** and edit the following fields:

Shipping Prices: Choose **Calculate them for me**

Origin ZIP code: Enter the zip code you will be shipping packages from

Processing Time: Enter how long it will take you to prepare, package, and put the package in the mail. Choose the fastest processing time you can as fast shipping will help you attract more buyers. I have my setting at 1-2 business days, but I usually ship the following business day.

Where I'll ship: Here you can select the countries and regions you will ship to.

Shipping Services: Etsy automatically selects all options available, so you will need to deselect the ones you don't want. For items weighing under one pound, I choose *USPS First-Class Mail.* For boxes weighing over a pound, I choose *USPS Priority Mail.* If I am offering international shipping, I select *Standard International.* Note that *Media Mail* and *Parcel Select* are located under the *Advanced shipping services* tab.

Free Shipping: Etsy is a big proponent of offering "free" shipping, even offering to boost your listings if you at least offer "free" shipping on orders of $35 or more. However, as noted earlier, "free" shipping can get you into trouble if you aren't properly building the postage cost into the price of your items. I only offer "free" shipping on lightweight items. And even in those cases I only offer *Free domestic shipping*; I do not offer *Free international shipping*. The cost of international postage is simply too high for sellers to absorb. Otherwise, I charge shipping.

Depending on what you sell, you may be able to adjust your prices to meet the "free" shipping for orders of $35 or more. But don't bend to the pressure to offer "free" shipping if the costs are too much to absorb. If you sell larger items, it will be nearly impossible to offer free shipping, and that's okay. Most customers understand that while things like jewelry and stationary can ship for "free,", they know pottery and baskets cannot.

Check out what your competition is doing for their shipping. If everyone in your category charges shipping, then you won't have to worry about losing customers to another shop simply because of shipping charges. But if the majority of sellers in your category are offering "free" shipping, it will be hard to attract buyers if you don't, too.

Handling Fee: Etsy allows sellers to charge buyers a handling fee. However, this is something I avoid. With the rising supply costs and postage rates, it's hard enough to price items competitively. Adding a handling charge will only push your prices higher, which can turn off potential shoppers. I recommend adding your packing costs to the price of your item as much as possible.

Profile Name: As a crafter, it's likely many of your products will weigh and ship the same. Creating a *Profile name* will make listing new products faster. For example, if you sell jewelry and offer "free" shipping, you could name the profile "Free Jewelry Shipping." On the other hand, if you sell pottery of different weights, you could name your profiles "2 Pound Pottery," "3 Pound Pottery," and so on. Then when you ship new pieces, you can simply choose the profile that matches the weight of the package.

Item Weight & Size: Once you've finished filling out the *Shipping* options section, you will next need to enter the weight and size of the package. Using the soap set example from earlier, which, when placed in a box, weighed 1 pound 4 ounces. That means you enter 1 pound 4 ounces into the package weight, right?

WRONG!

When you are dealing with weights above a pound (remember, sixteen ounces or less can go via *First Class*; and since the soaps are not books, they cannot go via *Media Mail*), you do NOT need to know the EXACT weight; you only need to know the RANGE between pounds. Understanding that you only need to know the RANGE will make your shipping process go much more smoothly.

Here's the Trick: If you know the item you are selling with ship within the one-to-two-pound range, you simply enter 2 lbs 0 oz under *Item weight and size*. By entering in two pounds, it will cover the postage for items that weigh in the one-to-two-pound range when shipped, including our soap example, which weighs 1 pound 4 ounces.

Remember that once you get over a pound, packages ship in pound ranges. One to two pounds, two to three pounds, etc. The trick is to just enter the highest of the two ranges. For packages that weigh between one and two pounds, you enter in two pounds. For packages that weigh between two and three pounds, you enter in three pounds.

See how easy it is when you only need to know the weight RANGE? One to two pounds, two to three pounds, three to four pounds, etc. When an item is being shipped via *Parcel Select, Priority Mail,* or *Media Mail,* you only need to know the RANGE of weight. There is no need to worry about being exact down to the ounce. Just round it up to the largest pound, and you are good to go!

As I mentioned earlier, I mentally add three ounces to small packages to account for packing materials. Yes, packing paper, newspaper, bubble wrap, packing peanuts, enclosures, and tape will add additional weight to the shipment. For example, let's say you are selling a set of handmade bath bombs. In a shipping box, they weigh in at 1 pound 6 ounces. I would mentally note the weight as 1 pound 9 ounces to account for packing materials that will be added later. However, you still wouldn't put in the exact weight. You would only need to round up to two pounds.

But what about packages that weigh less than one pound? While packages over one pound are categorized in ranges of pounds for Media, Parcel, and Priority, packages under 16 ounces have their own ranges for First Class Mail: 1-4 ounces, 5-8 ounces, 9-12 ounces, and 13-16 ounces. So you must get the exact ounces for First Class, right?

Not really! As with rounding up for Media, Parcel, and Priority, you want to round up for First Class. Let's say you sell custom beaded bracelets that you package in small boxes. When the box is placed in a padded bubble mailer, the weight comes out to be 10 ounces. That means it falls into the 9-12 ounce range. Therefore, you would want to round up and enter 12 ounces.

I sometimes ship items that when packaged, are hovering right at the 4-ounce weight. To be safe, I round it up to 8 ounces. That way if the Post Office's scale weighs it just a smidge heavier, I'm safe.

Here's a chart for easy reference:

First Class:

- 1-4 ounces
- 5-8 ounces
- 9-12 ounces

- 13-16 ounces

Media, Parcel & Priority:

- 1-2 pounds
- 2-3 pounds
- 4-5 pounds
- 5-6 pounds

Note that larger breakables often need more packing materials than the three-ounce buffer will provide. So while my three-ounce trick works for small items, if I'm shipping something in a 12x12x12-inch box that will need bubble wrap, packing peanuts, and packing paper, I will likely need to bump the package into the next weight range. This is why it is so important to weigh your items in a box similar to what it will ship in and to figure out how much extra materials will be used. You can do this by doing mockups on every size of your product.

Using the pottery example from earlier, if you are selling five different sizes of bowl, package up each on to get a better idea of the shipping weight. You may think the largest bowl you have is 5 pounds, but once you package it with packing materials, you realize the weight is close to 7 pounds. A 1-2 pound difference can mean several extra dollars, depending on where the order is shipping to.

Item Size (when packed): The final field to fill out for Etsy shipping is *Item size*. This is an optional field and one you do not have to worry about unless your package is oversized. Packages that measure OVER 36 inches in length and girth combined are oversized. Basically, this means that boxes measuring OVER 12 x 12 x12 inches are oversized and will likely need to shop via *Parcel*. Any size box under that is standard size. And you don't need to enter in standard sizes.

Let's revisit our pottery example. If you have five different bowl sizes and the first four all fit in the *Large Priority Mail* box, they are standard size. You do not need to enter the box dimensions for those sizes. But let's say your largest bowl have to ship in a 14 x 14 x 14 and weighs 10 pounds. Etsy will automatically tell you that you can ship that size doesn't qualify for international shipping. And while it will allow you to choose *Priority* as an option, once your listing goes live, you will see that the cost to ship via *Priority* is much higher than *Parcel.* In this instance, it's best to give your customers a choice by offering both. Etsy will show them the cost to ship the item via *Parcel* versus *Priority,* and they can choose which they want to pay for.

Printing Labels: An order has come in! It's time to print the shipping label and send the package to the customer.

To find new orders, go to your *Etsy Shop Manager* by clicking on the small "store" icon at the top of the page. On the left side of the page, you'll see a bar of options. Look for the orange circle with a number in it next to **Orders & Shipping** - this indicates that you have orders to ship. Click on *Orders & Shipping* to view them.

Note that you can print shipping labels in bulk by selecting all the orders. However, let's go through the process of shipping one order at a time. The first time you ship anything can be stressful since it's a new process, but it will become second nature once you've shipped out a few orders.

All your orders will be in one section on this page, with each order shown inside a light box. Hover your mouse over the box to shadow it, and click anywhere in the shadowed area to open a pop-up window.

Click on **Get shipping labels**. The shipping details, such as weight and postage method, that you entered when creating the listing have already been preselected. However, if you need to change anything, such as the package type, weight, box size, or delivery service, you can do so here.

TIP: Even though you didn't need to enter a package size when creating your listing, sometimes Etsy will require it when printing the actual label. If the package is shipping within the United States via Priority Mail, Media Mail, or Parcel Select, the size of the box only matters if it is over 36 inches combined. Boxes measuring 12x12x12 inches or less do not need exact measurements, so, for domestic shipments, you can put any measurements you want. However, if you can enter the exact measurements, there is no reason not to. Most boxes come printed with their measurements on the bottom. If you're shipping internationally, exact measurements may be necessary to calculate the correct shipping cost.

Once everything on the screen is correct, click **Review**. A new screen will pop up showing you the cost of the label you're about to purchase. This cost will be added to your Etsy bill, and Etsy will automatically deduct it from your balance.

Click on the **Purchase** icon. A pop-up screen will appear. Click on **Print shipping labels** and then click on the **Print** icon on the screen. Another pop-up screen with the label will appear. Choose the printer you want to print the label from, and then click **Print.**

Once the label has been printed, close the screen. You'll now be back on the screen where you choose *Print shipping labels.* You'll also see an option to **Print packing slips.** I like to print packing slips because they help me stay organized when I'm printing several orders at once, and I think including them in orders gives a professional touch to my business. But the choice to do so is completely up to you.

After printing the label and packing slip, you can go ahead and package your order!

TIP: If you need to reprint or redo any shipping label for any reason, you can do so by going back to the *Orders & Shipping* section and clicking on the *Completed Orders* tab. Here, you'll see all the orders for which you've printed labels. If you need to refund a label and reprint it, whether because the label didn't print correctly or you misplaced it, simply click on the *Refund* link under the tracking number. Etsy will ask you why you want to refund the label. You can then pay for and print a new label. It will take a few days, but you'll eventually be refunded the cost of the first label.

Packing Orders: Once you have printed the shipping label, you need to package the order. The amount of packing materials you will need depends on what you are selling. If you sell textiles such as clothing, tote bags, and tea towels, you can easily ship those in poly mailing bags with no extra packaging. You simply close up the bag and attach the shipping labels. Jewelry should be put into a protective bag or box but can then be placed inside a small bubble mail envelope without extra padding. Paper items such as cards and stickers should be placed in a cardboard mailer to prevent them from being bent during shipping.

However, for larger, breakable items, it isn't enough to put the item into a box by itself. You need to protect the item when it is transported during the shipping process.

Box-In-A-Box: Experienced online sellers often talk about the *box-in-a-box* method for shipping. This technique involves creating a boxlike barrier between your product and the shipping box to protect it during transit. If you're a frequent online shopper, you've probably received boxes in various states of disarray. The *box-in-a-box* method helps prevent damage to your product caused by damage to the shipping box itself. This method is especially important if you're shipping breakable items such as pottery and ceramics, or items that can easily dent.

To use the *box-in-a-box* method for breakable items, start by wrapping your item in bubble wrap. I recommend that you use at least two layers of bubble wrap for added protection, more if the item is glass or porcelain. Then, use cardboard rolls, which you can purchase on Amazon, to wrap around the bubble wrap. This creates a box-like barrier around your item. Use plenty of packing materials, such as packing peanuts, shredded paper, and/or packing paper, to secure the item in the shipping box.

My test for if an item is packaged well is to shake the box. If nothing rattles around, it's packaged well. If I can feel the item shifting, I open up the box and put more packing material inside. Delivery people often throw boxes into their trucks and onto porches, so, in my opinion, you can't really overpack an order!

Here are some additional tips for packing Etsy orders, specifically crafts:

Choose the Right Box: Make sure you choose a box that is sturdy enough to protect your items during shipping. If you're shipping delicate or fragile items, use the box-in-a-box method and also add in extra padding. While it's fine to repurpose clean boxes, be sure the boxes are good for shipping breakables. For example, Amazon shipping boxes tend to by very lightweight. While they can be repurposed for some items, they aren't always the best choice for shipping glass or pottery.

Wrap, Wrap, Wrap: Wrap your items in bubble wrap or packing paper to prevent them from moving around in the box during shipping. You can also use tissue paper or shredded paper for extra cushioning on items that aren't in danger of breaking. Cardboard rolls also provide an added layer of protection. I save every bit of clean packing material I get in my own online shopping orders to reuse for shipping the items I sell.

Add a Personal Touch: Consider adding a handwritten note or a pre-printed thank you card along with a small freebie to thank your customer for their purchase. I like to include the packing slip that I printed from Etsy along with a free sticker or magnet that features my shop URL. I find that stickers and magnets are a better choice than regular cards as buyers will use them rather than throw them away.

Use Clear Tape: Use clear shipping tape (remember, the best deals are at Sam's Club and Costco, although you can also find good prices on Amazon) to seal the box securely. Make sure to tape all the seams and edges to prevent the box from coming apart during shipping. If you are using a label you printed out on paper, it is okay to put some clear tape over the edges of the shipping label, but don't put tape over the bar code as it can interfere with the Post Office being able to scan your package into their system.

Do Not Wrap Up the Box: New sellers sometimes make the mistake of wrapping their boxes in brown paper. Not only is this a waste of time and money, but it is also against postal guidelines as the edges of the paper can get stuck in the sorting machines. If you are repurposing a box and want to cover up printing that is on it, consider using brown packing tape or stickers. If the package is being shipped via Priority Mail, you can use the free Priority Mail stickers from the Post Office to cover things up.

Mailing Orders: Once you've secured the shipping label to your package, it's time to get it into the hands of the USPS. There are two ways to do this: you can either drive your packages to your local Post Office or schedule a free Carrier Pickup.

If you choose to take your packages to the Post Office, you have a couple of options. You can wait in line and have your packages scanned in, or you can take them to the loading dock around the back of the building to unload them without having to wait in line. However, every

Post Office location has its own policies, so make sure to ask before leaving your packages.

If you only have a few packages, you may be able to leave them inside at the counter without having to wait in line. Again, ask what's easiest for the employees and be accommodating. Remember, these people are an essential part of your business, and being kind and polite can go a long way.

Your second option is to schedule a free pickup from your postal carrier. Scheduling a free Carrier Pickup from the USPS is a great option for online sellers who have a large number of packages or who are unable to make it to the Post Office during business hours. To schedule a pickup, visit tool.usps.com/schedule-pickup-steps. Note that you need to have at least one *First Class* or *Priority* package to request a free pickup. If all of your packages are shipping via *Media* or *Parcel,* you will have to take them to the Post Office yourself.

You can schedule package pickups Monday through Saturday. If you have a small number of packages, your regular carrier will likely collect them. However, if you have a large number of outgoing orders, the Post Office may send a mail truck out to pick them up. You must be prepared for your packages to be picked up at any time. I have a deck box on my porch where I put my outgoing packages. This protects them from the elements as well as from being stolen. I leave a note on my mailbox directing whoever is picking up the packages as to where they are.

PRO TIP: If you have a lot of outgoing Etsy orders for your USPS carrier to collect, and if you are getting numerous packages of supplies to run your shop, consider leaving snacks out for your delivery drivers. I have a box filled with pre-packed candy bars, chips, and cookies that I leave out for those who collect and deliver packages to my home. I buy these snacks in bulk from Sam's Club. All of the delivery people who come to my house appreciate these!

Tracking: Etsy will notify the customer when their package has shipped. There is no need to message your customer directly unless there is an issue with their order. If you printed the shipping label on Etsy, the tracking for the package will automatically upload for both you and your customer.

And that's it! You have shipped your first Etsy order! Trust me that after you have shipped out a few packages, the process will become easier. Once the package has been scanned in at your buyer's location, Etsy will release the funds from the sale to your account. And when you start to see your Etsy balance build, you'll wonder why you waited so long to sell your crafts online!

CHAPTER SIX: MARKETING YOUR ETSY SHOP

If you have been selling your crafts locally, you may already have some advertising in place. However, to grow your business online, you will need to ramp up your efforts. Fortunately, marketing your crafts online is easy thanks to social media platforms. And in many cases, these options are also free.

In this chapter, we'll discuss the various social media sites and how you can utilize each to drive traffic to your Etsy shop. We'll also talk about some paid options you can consider. But first, just another reminder that the best thing you can do to advertise your business is to maximize Etsy SEO.

Are you tired of me harping on Etsy SEO? If you are, I don't blame you. But it is the best thing you can do to drive traffic to your Etsy shop and make sales. Remember that SEO (Search Engine Optimization) involves repeating relevant keywords in your titles, descriptions, tags, and shop sections. This repetition of keywords tells Etsy that they need to focus on those keywords when putting your items into their search algorithm.

When done effectively, SEO can help your Etsy products to rank higher in search results and increase the chances of them being seen by potential customers. And effective use of SEO can eliminate the need to run expensive Etsy Ads. Once I mastered Etsy SEO, I stopped using Etsy Ads, which are the ads you pay for whenever someone clicks on them. I do, however, opt into Etsy Off-Site Ads as I only pay for those ads when a click leads to a sale.

It can't be said enough that maximizing Etsy SEO is the number one tool you must utilize to bring customers to your shop. Researching the best keywords for your products and using those keywords in your titles, descriptions, tags, shop sections, and even in areas where you can customize your shop's announcements and information will tell Etsy that they need to be pushing your products to customers searching those keywords.

Is it annoying that you can't just write a good title and be done with the listing? Yes. Is it tempting to just focus on a keyword-loaded title and call it a day the same way Amazon, eBay, and Poshmark sellers do with their listings? Yes. But unfortunately, this isn't the reality of selling on Etsy. Repeating the most important keywords that pertain to your listings is the best thing you can do to bring shoppers to your listings and turn those shoppers into paying customers.

Although SEO plays a significant role in helping customers discover your products on platforms like Etsy and Google, there are additional strategies you can utilize to drive traffic to your Etsy store. The good news is that most of these tactics are not only fast and easy but also free. This is because these methods involve leveraging social media platforms to grow your business.

Back in the early days of e-commerce, there were only a handful of shopping websites available, and customers had limited options for purchasing items online. When I started selling online, eBay and Amazon were the only online shopping websites. I was able to easily sell on both platforms for several years as there was little competition. Since customers had only two choices when it came to online shopping, I didn't have to compete for their attention. Shoppers came to me because I was one of the few online sellers. I didn't even need to have the best product pictures, titles, or descriptions. I could just take a couple of photos and list products for sale without doing any advertising.

However, the e-commerce landscape has changed significantly since I began selling online in 2005. There are now thousands of online shopping websites available. Every single brand and retail store has its e-commerce website, and numerous "reselling" platforms have emerged alongside eBay and Amazon, including Etsy, Poshmark, Mercari, Facebook Marketplace, TikTok Shops, and WhatNot. Not to mention small brands and individually sellers who create their own websites through Shopify and Wix to sell directly to customers. This increase in competition means that simply listing products for sale online is no longer enough to make sales.

Etsy is an especially competitive marketplace. It is no longer just for crafters. Vintage and antique sellers, sticker shops, print-on-demand drop shipping, and digital downloads are all a huge part of Etsy's offerings. That means that you as a seller are not only competing against other crafters but all of the other shops on Etsy.

For instance, if you sell custom water bottles, you will be competing with shops that sell digital water bottle wraps that customers can download, print, and apply to their own water bottles. Or sellers who use third-party providers to print and ship their water bottle designs straight to customers. While you may be the only water bottle crafter in your local area, you will find hundreds of similar shops on Etsy.

Because so many people are now selling on Etsy, it is important to think of your Etsy shop as a brand. The category and niches you focus on, the handmade items you create, and the aesthetic of your items should all have a cohesive look and theme that contributes to your brand identity. If you sell handmade jewelry, you'll likely be using silver and gold colors for not only your products but also the overall look of your shop. If you are selling hand-carved wooden children's toys, your shop may utilize bright colors that appeal to kids.

Once you have mastered Etsy SEO and have done all you can to bring in shoppers who are already on Etsy, you can turn your attention to bringing in customers from other websites. And the first place you will want to start is on Facebook.

Facebook: To establish your craft's brand, you must create a Facebook page. Facebook has a user base of nearly 3 billion people around the world, making it the ideal platform for reaching new customers. Not only is Facebook free to use, but it's also user-friendly. While other social media sites, like TikTok, are gaining momentum, Facebook remains the top choice for businesses as you can reach an older audience of users who have more disposable income to spend on things such as crafts.

To use Facebook to drive traffic to your Etsy store, you'll need to create a **Facebook Business Page,** which is different from a personal Facebook page. With a personal Facebook page, you receive friend requests from family and acquaintances. You have the option of keeping your profile entirely private, and you don't need to censor yourself because only those you approve as "friends" can see your posts.

However, a *Facebook Business Page* is separate from a personal account. Rather than people "friending" you, they will instead need to "like" your page to "follow" you. You need this distinction to separate your personal life from your business, not only to build your brand but to protect your privacy. While you may enjoy discussing politics and religion on your personal Facebook page, you want to refrain from these sometimes-controversial topics when it comes to your business. A business page also protects the privacy of your personal friends and family as customers won't see their information.

A *Facebook Business Page* enables you to advertise your products, provide business updates, and engage with your customers. You can easily link your Etsy shop to your Facebook page, which will allow users to click through to your store.

To create a *Facebook Business Page,* you first need to have a personal Facebook account. From there you simply:

1. Go to facebook.com/about/pages
2. Log in to your personal Facebook account (even if you were already logged in, Facebook's system will usually have you reenter your login information to confirm your identity)
3. Follow the prompts to create a new business page

The first decision you will need to make is to name your page. I currently have several Facebook pages, including one for my Etsy shop. My Etsy shop's Facebook page name is *Jean Lee Publishing,* which matches my Etsy shop name.

As you create additional social media accounts related to your craft business, it's important to make sure that they all have the same name to establish a cohesive online presence. You will want all your social media account names to match or closely match your Etsy shop name.

For example, I sell journals, planners, notebooks, and adult coloring books on Amazon through their self-publishing platform, Amazon KDP. My pen name for those products is Jean Lee Publishing. I decided to name my Etsy shop the same so that I could create different products under one "brand name," which has enabled me to have a dedicated website, JeanLeePublishing.com, where customers can choose to visit my Etsy shop or Amazon storefront.

The biggest benefit of having one brand name is that it allows me to have one social media handle for both platforms. Since all of my products fall under the "stationery" category, it made sense for me to focus on combing all of my items together under one name. By directing customers to JeanLeePublishing.com, they can see all of the stationery products I sell and click through to the ones they are most interested in.

After you have created a Facebook business account, Facebook will prompt you to personalize your page by:

1. **Adding a profile picture:** This is the image that will appear next to your page name and posts. You want to use the same profile picture for your Facebook page that you use for your Etsy shop. Most Etsy sellers choose their shop's logo as their profile picture.

2. **Adding a banner:** This is the large image that appears at the top of your Facebook page. You can create a custom banner on a site like Canva, which has templates already made for Facebook banners. If this type of graphics work isn't something you are comfortable making, you can hire a designer on a site such as Fiverr.com who can create banners and any other graphics you need.

3. **Customizing your page's tabs:** Facebook allows you to add various tabs to your page, such as an events calendar or a shop tab, including linking your Etsy shop right on your page.

Be sure to complete the **About** section on your Facebook business page to provide followers with information about your Etsy shop. Include details about your products, who your target audience is, and why you started your business in the first place. While you can post a bit of personal information, such as if you have a spouse, children, your hobbies, and such, be careful about posting too many intimate details. Remember that you want to guard your privacy and that of your family as well as keep your personal life separate from your business.

Because you are selling handmade items, you may want to keep communication open on your Facebook page to local customers and event organizers. You can do this by providing a phone number. However, if you aren't comfortable posting your phone number online, you can add an email address. In fact, if you don't already have a dedicated email address for your business, you should create one for free through Google. If you already have a Gmail account, you can create additional email addresses under it. You can also allow people to contact you via Facebook Messenger, where you can then decide if you are comfortable providing them with a direct phone number of email.

If you are only selling your wares on Etsy, then there is no reason for you to provide a phone number or email address. Your number one goal should be to drive traffic to your Etsy shop. Therefore, the link to your Etsy shop should be the main link to your showcase on all of your social media platforms.

Page Category: Several Facebook categories may be relevant for a crafting business, and Facebook allows you to select three for your business page. I recommend the following:

1. **Arts & Crafts**
2. **Product/Service**
3. **Shopping & Retail**

While *Arts & Crafts* is the most important category you want to choose, you also want to choose two additional categories so that your Facebook page is visible to as many people as possible. *Product/Service* and *Shopping & Retail* are the two most logical categories to add as they are geared towards shoppers.

The goal is to get Facebook users to "like" your page. And when they "like" your page, Facebook will then show their friends and family your page. This method of gaining followers through "likes" is how you build your Facebook following, which will then translate into bringing more people to your Etsy shop. Note that you can also change categories at any time if necessary.

Once you've chosen your page's categories, you will want to personalize your Facebook business page by editing the URL to reflect the name of your page. Remember that you want to name your page the same as your Etsy shop or close to it. This will make it easier for users to find and follow your page, as well as establish a cohesive online presence.

To **change the username** of your page, follow these steps:

1. Go to your Facebook page and click on the **About** tab.
2. Click on the **Edit** button next to the **Page Info** section.
3. Scroll down to the **Username** field and click on the **Create** button.
4. Enter the desired username and click **Save.**

Once you have saved your username, your Facebook URL will be updated to reflect the name of your page. You can share this URL with customers and promote it on your other social media platforms and online listings to drive traffic to your Facebook page and increase engagement with your brand. A simple method for this is to direct people to find you on Facebook using the @ symbol. For example, my Facebook page is @jeanleepublishing. Entering @jeanleepublishing into the Facebook search bar will take you directly to my page.

The **About** section of your Facebook page offers several different fields that you can fill out. Facebook prompts will walk you through this section. However, note that you don't have to complete any of these sections right away or at all if you don't want to. If the main goal is to drive traffic to your Etsy shop, then your Etsy link is the most important link you want on your page.

Once you have set up your Facebook business page, you need to start building your audience by getting people to "like" your page. Facebook will prompt you to invite friends and family from your personal account to "like" your new page and most of the people you are connected with will give your page a follow. However, remember that you can't expect your friends and family to buy from you. To build a business, you need to reach beyond your immediate circle.

While creating a Facebook business page is free, there are some paid options that Facebook offers to help grow your business. Facebook Ads allow you to target specific groups of people who may be interested in your products and encourage them to "like" your page to click through to your Etsy shop.

To create a Facebook ad:

1. Go to your Facebook business page and click on the **Create** button at the top of the page.
2. From the drop-down menu, select **Ad** to create a new ad campaign.
3. **Choose your ad objective.** Facebook offers a range of ad objectives to choose from, including "Website Visits," "Conversions," "Product Catalog Sales," and more. I recommend "Website Visits" because, after all, the goal is to bring customers to your Etsy shop.
4. **Set up your targeting options.** Facebook allows you to target specific groups of people based on demographics, interests, behaviors, and more. Use the targeting options to narrow down your audience to the people most likely to be interested in your products. You can do this by typing in keywords that relate to your products.
5. **Select your ad placements.** You can choose to show your ad on Facebook, Instagram, or both, as well as on other

platforms such as "Audience Network" and "Marketplace." I choose all options so that my ad has the widest reach.

6. **Set your budget and schedule.** Decide how much you want to spend on your ad campaign and over what period. You can choose to run your ad continuously or set specific start and end dates. I usually start with $5 a day to test the ad.

7. **Create your ad.** Use the ad creation tools to design your ad, including the ad format, images, text, and call-to-action (CTA) button. You can choose from a variety of ad formats, including single images, carousels, and videos. I recommend adding a few of your best-selling product photos.

8. **Review and submit your ad.** Once you have finished creating your ad, review all the details to make sure everything is correct. When you are ready, click **Submit** to create your ad campaign.

The **Boost Post** feature on Facebook is another paid advertising tool that allows you to promote a specific post from your Facebook business page to a larger audience. This is an easier method than creating an ad from scratch. For example, I often share direct links to new products on my Facebook page. I can then "boost" that specific post rather than create an ad from scratch.

To **boost a post from your Facebook business page**, follow these steps:

1. Go to your Facebook business page and find the post that you want to promote.

2. Click on the **Boost Post** button below the post.

3. **Select your target audience.** You can choose to show your boosted post to people who already like your page, to a specific group of people based on demographics and interests, or to a custom audience that you define. I usually choose to

have the post shown to people who "like" my page and their friends and family. This way the people they are connected to will see that their friend or family member "likes" my business, which can encourage them to check it out.

4. **Set your budget and duration**. Decide how much you want to spend on your boosted post and over what period. You can choose to boost your post for as little as $1 per day or as much as you want. I like to choose a seven-day option with a budget of no more than $35 ($5 per day) to test how the ad performs.

5. **Review and boost your post.** Once you have finished setting up your boosted post, review all the details to make sure everything is correct. When you are ready, click **Boost** to promote your post.

So, you have set up a Facebook page for your business and have started getting people to "like" it. Now you need to commit to posting regular content on your page to keep your followers engaged. Creating engagement isn't just about seeing followers see your posts but also interacting with them by clicking the "thumbs up" button, leaving comments, or sharing your posts on their Facebook feeds to get their friends and family to like your page, too.

I always share my newest listings directly to my Facebook page, which Etsy makes easy to do. To **share an Etsy listing on your Facebook page**, follow these steps:

1. Go to your Etsy shop and find the listing that you want to share.
2. Click on the **Share** button below the listing.
3. Select **Facebook** from the drop-down menu.
4. A pop-up window will appear, asking you to log in to your Facebook account. Enter your login credentials and click **Log**

In.

5. A new window will appear, allowing you to customize the message that will be posted to your Facebook page along with the listing. You can add a message or simply leave the default message.

6. When you are ready, click **Post to Facebook** to share the listing on your Facebook page.

In addition to promoting your Etsy listings on Facebook, find other ways to engage with your followers. You can do this by posting updates about new product launches, sharing your best-selling products for a particular week or month, running polls, doing giveaways, or sharing relevant information such as deadlines for holiday orders. Even posting holiday messages and reminders about events is an easy way to keep your page active.

Remember that when people engage with your Facebook posts, Facebook may show the engagement in that person's feed so that their friends can see it. And those friends, seeing that they know someone who follows your page, may decide to follow your page, too. Therefore, it is important to keep your posts positive and avoid posting about controversial or offensive topics. In other words, unless you are selling religious or political-themed products, avoid those two topics. The goal of your business page is to attract customers and make money. Posting about sensitive subjects can turn people away.

However, that's not to say you can't have non-business content on your Facebook business page. Sharing a picture of your lunch while you take a break from designing or posting a meme related to your niche can often bring more engagement than posting a new listing. A picture of your pet, a funny quote, or simply wishing your customers a "happy-whatever-holiday-it-is" can go a long way toward building rapport with your followers. And the more rapport you have with your followers, the more likely they are to turn into customers.

Facebook Groups: As your business grows, you may decide to create a special Facebook group just for your Etsy shop customers. I have a Facebook group for my Etsy sticker shop that lets me connect with my best customers. They help me narrow down new sticker designs and get the first notification of new products. I reward their loyalty with special discount codes.

To **start a Facebook group:**

1. Log into Facebook and navigate to your business page.
2. In the top right corner of your page, click the **Create Group** button.
3. Select either **Close** (a private group that only members can access), **Secret** (an even more private group that only members can see and that doesn't appear in search results), or **Public** (a group that anyone can see and join). I have my group set to private so that Facebook users can see it but only members can see what is being posted. Since I post exclusive discount codes in the group, I want to make sure only members can see those posts.
4. Choose a **name and description** that accurately represents your business and the purpose of the group. I recommend selecting a name that matches up with your Etsy shop. My Etsy sticker shop is "Jean Lee Publishing," and my Facebook group is "Jean Lee's Sticker Club."
5. You can **invite members** by searching for Facebook users, adding email addresses, or inviting members from your business page.
6. You can **customize group settings** such as who can post and comment, who can see the group, and who can be added as a

     member.
7. When you're ready, click the **Create** button to launch your group. You can start posting updates and engaging with members right away.

It's hard to start a group until you have people following your Facebook page. And having a group isn't a necessity for any business. As your business grows and you build up a loyal customer base, it may be something to consider, especially if you are in a niche where you have the potential for repeat customers. It's also a great idea if you sell your crafts locally and accept online orders outside of Etsy.

Twitter: Like Facebook, Twitter is another free social media platform that you can use to promote your Etsy shop. With Twitter, you can share short updates, called "tweets," with your followers and engage with them through **@replies** and **#hashtags.**

If you don't already have a Twitter account, you can create one for free at Twitter.com. Note that if you have an existing personal Twitter account that you are active on, you may want to consider creating a separate account for your Etsy business to keep your personal and professional lives separate. You can create multiple Twitter accounts; you just need to use separate email addresses.

Remember as you are creating social media pages for your Etsy shop to use the same handle for your Twitter account as you have for your Etsy shop and Facebook page to create a consistent online presence for your business. This will make it easier for people to find and follow you across different platforms and helps in building your brand.

Twitter limits their "tweets" to 280 characters or less. Etsy makes it easy to share your listings on Twitter by including a share button in all active listings. To use the Twitter share button, simply click on it within a listing, and a new window will open on Twitter with the title of your listing and the direct link to it already populated. You can send the "tweet" as is or customize the message as well as add hashtags.

Hashtags (marked as such with the # sign) are a way to categorize and organize content on social media platforms, especially on Twitter. In fact, I find that hashtags are more useful on Twitter than on any other platform as users are more accustomed to using them there than on other sites. Twitter users can follow their favorite hashtags to keep up with the posts they are most interested in seeing.

Adding hashtags to your "tweets" is an easy way to increase the chance of your posts being found by interested shoppers. By adding relevant hashtags to your tweets, you are making it easier for people to discover your Etsy business and perhaps buy your items.

For example, let's say you have a handmade candle Etsy shop. When you click on the Twitter icon in your Etsy listing, your title and the link to the listing will automatically populate to Twitter. If there is room to add more text, you can add hashtags such as #etsy, #etsyshop, #candles, and #handmade. If the candle is for a specific occasion or holiday, such as a wedding candle or a Christmas candle, add hashtags to represent those events. These hashtags will help your tweet show up in searches for these topics, meaning they will show up for Twitter users following those hashtags.

It's important not to overuse hashtags or use ones that are not relevant to your business. This can make your tweets seem spammy and could turn people off. Instead, choose around five relevant hashtags that accurately describe your business and the products you are selling. While the bridal category is huge on Etsy, don't use the hashtag #bridal in your listings if you sell handmade baby bibs.

As with sharing your Facebook page with customers, you also want to share your Twitter handle, both online and offline, to encourage them to follow you on the platform. Including your Twitter handle in your other social media profiles and on any other promotional materials will help your customers find you. The @ symbol allows you to easily share your Twitter handle as typing it into Twitter's search bar will take users to your profile.

One way to build up your followers on Twitter is to follow other Twitter users and engage with their content. Some users follow everyone who follows them, which can help increase your follower count. You can also use Twitter's @reply and retweet features to engage with other users and share their content with your followers. This can help build relationships and expose your content to a wider audience. However, avoid connecting with other Etsy sellers who sell the same items you do to avoid competition.

Instagram: Like Facebook, Instagram is a social media platform that allows users to share photos and videos and engage with their followers. In fact, Facebook's parent company META owns both Facebook and Instagram, so there is some built-in overlap between the two sites, specifically when it comes to advertising.

PRO TIP: Because Facebook owns Instagram, you can connect your accounts so that your Instagram posts will automatically share to your Facebook business page. This is a great time saver as you don't have to create two different posts for each site. Post once on Instagram and the post will share on Facebook automatically.

There are several features on Instagram that you can use to share your content about your Etsy shop:

Instagram Posts: *Instagram Posts* are static photos that you share on your profile. They are visible to all your followers and remain on your profile indefinitely unless you delete them. *Instagram Posts* are an easy way to share the images of your products, which is easy to do by simply reposting the same images to Instagram that you use in your Etsy listings.

Instagram Stories: *Instagram Stories* are photos or videos that you share on your profile that disappear after 24 hours. *Instagram Stories* are a good way to share behind-the-scenes glimpses of your business, sneak peeks of new products, or more personal content that you may want to share with your followers but that doesn't need to remain on your profile indefinitely.

For example, while I want pictures of my products to always appear on my profile page, I don't need to permanently save a short video of me packing an order. Note that you can also share your static posts to your stories to make sure those posts get maximum exposure.

Instagram Reels: *Instagram Reels* allows users to create and share short video clips of up to one minute and thirty seconds that can be edited with music, effects, and custom text. *Instagram Reels* is a good way to create and share fun content that highlights your products. As with static posts, you can also share *Instagram Reels* to your *Instagram Stories.*

In addition to using Instagram to promote your Etsy listings, you can also use the platform to connect with your customers on a more personal level by sharing photos that may not always relate directly to your business. For example, you can post photos of your office, products you are working on, and other behind-the-scenes glimpses of your shop. Creating handmade crafts gives you a lot of potential content to share, much more so than sellers of digital products or even antiques as so much goes into the creation of homemade goods.

Instagram is very much a visual platform, so sharing photos of your pets, meals, or other fun snapshots can give your followers a more personal look at your life. Remember, however, that you are using

Instagram to promote your Etsy shop. Just as with your other social media business pages, you should avoid sharing controversial or offensive content.

Just as you use hashtags on Twitter, they are also a useful tool on Instagram. Make sure to use hashtags that are relevant to your business and the content you are sharing. This will help ensure that your posts are seen by users who are interested in what you are selling. As an Etsy handmade shop, stick to hashtags related to the niche and products you are selling. Many people will use hashtags that have nothing to do with their Etsy shop to be seen by more users. But this can backfire if those users are annoyed seeing your content in their feed and react negatively by leaving angry comments under your posts.

Using popular hashtags can help increase the visibility of your content but using too many popular hashtags can make it harder for your content to stand out. Consider using a mix of hashtags to balance visibility and relevance. For example, you want to use the hashtags #etsy and #etsyshop in most of your Instagram posts. But also add hashtags of the theme of the products you are posting about. If you are sharing listings about custom Father's Day greeting cards, use hashtags such as #dad, #fathersday, and #giftsfordad to reach people who are searching for Father's Day gift ideas.

Narrowing down the hashtags you want to include can be a challenge as there are so many potential options. For instance, if you are selling personalized baby onesies, you could include any of these hashtags

- #etsy
- #etsyshop
- #newbaby
- #babyonesies
- #babyfashion
- #babyshowergift

- #cutebabyclothes
- #babyboyonesie
- #babygirlonesie
- #babyoutfit
- #newmom
- #babystyle
- #babiesofinstagram
- #instababy
- #babylove
- #babyessentials
- #babyootd
- #babywardrobe
- #babystuff
- #babyproducts

Utilizing a site such as EtsyCheck or eRank can help you find the best hashtags to use. I like to use a mix of popular and more niche hashtags to reach the widest audience possible. I use both EtsyCheck and eRank to find keywords for my listings and hashtags for my social media, along with researching what products are trending on Etsy. I keep a list of hashtags in the Notes section of my iPhone to easily copy and paste relevant hashtags to my Instagram posts.

Another way to grow your Instagram following is to connect with other Etsy sellers. You can find fellow Etsy shops using the hashtags #etsyshop and #etsyseller. Note, however, that as with Twitter, you want to avoid makers on Instagram who sell the same items you do. If you hand-poured soy candles, you want to steer clear of other soy candle makers. However, there are so many different sellers on Etsy that it won't be hard for you to find other crafters to follow. And if you follow them, they may follow you back, especially if you interact with their posts.

Linking Your Shop: While you can add a live clickable website link to your Instagram profile, you cannot add a live link to your Etsy shop in static Instagram posts, meaning if you add your Etsy shop's URL, it won't be clickable for users. Therefore, to drive traffic to your Etsy listings on Instagram in static posts, you need to include a message in the caption that directs your followers to your profile page, where they can find an active link to your Etsy shop. For example, you can write "Brand new embroidered Easter tea towels are now available in our Etsy shop! Follow the link in our profile @yourinstagramaccount to shop now!"

By including the @ symbol and your Instagram handle, you will create a clickable link that will take users to your profile page, where they can click on the link to your Etsy shop and browse your listings. While you can't add live links to static posts, you can add a live clickable link in your Instagram stories by using the **Link** option.

If you want to share multiple links on Instagram, not just the link to your Etsy shop, you will need to use a service like **Linktr.ee** to create a landing page that allows you to list all your links in one place. With a *Linktr.ee* page, you can add as many links as you like, allowing users to be able to access them all by clicking on the main *Linktr.ee* link in your Instagram profile. To see an example, visit my *Linktr.ee* page at **linktr.ee/anneckhart.**

Pinterest: Pinterest is a social media platform for sharing and discovering ideas and inspiration by "pinning" images and videos to virtual boards. Pinterest "boards" allow users to "pin" posts, similar to how one uses a bulletin board. Users create different "boards" for different categories and niches. Crafting is a huge category on Pinterest, so sharing your handmade items there just makes good business sense.

As with Facebook and Twitter, Etsy includes a share button in all active listings that makes it easy to share your listings on Pinterest. You can share your Etsy listings on specific boards that you have created that relate to your category and various niches. Let's say you make and sell handmade soaps. You could create one board for all of your soaps but also separate boards for different scent notes. I recommend starting a board that coincides with every one of your shop's sections.

As with the other social media platforms, you can use hashtags to make it easier for people to discover your Pinterest boards, although hashtags aren't used as much on Pinterest as they are on other sites. Pinterest is much more of a visual platform, so make sure the pictures you share are the best quality you have.

Finding content on Pinterest that coordinates with your products and re-pinning those posts as well as following their creators is another way to connect with not only other accounts but also the people who follow those accounts. However, as we've already discussed, avoid other makers who sell the same crafts you do to avoid unnecessary competition. Rather, search for content that relates to your niche. For instance, if you sell handmade quilts, follow boards about collecting and decorating with quilts as well as boards related to sewing.

If you do become active on Pinterest, be sure to share your Pinterest account with your customers and followers on other social media platforms and any promotional materials. You can easily add your Pinterest account to the links section of your Facebook business page as well as to your Linktr.ee if you have one.

TikTok: TikTok is a social media platform that allows users to create and share short videos, also referred to as "short-form content." TikTok began with a younger demographic but is slowly growing with users of all ages. On TikTok, users can create short videos (up to three minutes) that can be edited with music, effects, and other creative tools. From comedy skits and dances to personal stories and small business, there are TikTok videos for every interest.

Since TikTok relies on short-form videos, crafters have an immediate advantage when it comes to creating content. Filming clips of you making your items, using them, and packing them to ship to customers are easy ways to create videos based on what you are already doing.

The best part about TikTok is that it is for mobile devices, meaning you use your smartphone to film. TikTok offers several tutorials right on their app to walk you through the process. There are a lot of Etsy shop owners on TikTok, so it won't be hard for you to find other sellers to connect with. Remember, however, to avoid crafters who sell the same items you do.

There are two types of TikTok accounts to choose from: personal and business. A **TikTok personal account** is an account that is for, you guessed it, personal use. Most personal accounts aren't interested in growing a large following but are on TikTok just for fun. Many don't even post videos, they just have an account to scroll the site while being able to like, comment, and share their favorite clips.

A **TikTok business account**, however, is an account that is specifically designed for businesses, both small and large. Business accounts on TikTok have access to features and tools that are not available to personal accounts, such as analytics, advertising, and the ability to create and manage ads.

But the biggest benefit of a TikTok business account is that you can put a clickable URL in your profile. I have my Linktr.ee link in my TikTok business account profile, which will take people to a static page with all of my business links, including a link to my Etsy shop. Personal TikTok accounts can't put a clickable link in their profiles. And as with all social media platforms, your main goal should be driving traffic to your Etsy shop, which is much easier to do with a live link.

If you want to use TikTok to promote your Etsy business, you definitely want to create a TikTok business account. Note that you can create multiple TikTok pages within one account; if you already have a personal account, you can easily add a second account for your business. It's a simple process to switch back and forth between your multiple accounts without having to constantly log out and back in.

To create a TikTok business account for an Etsy shop, you will need to follow these steps:

1. **Download the TikTok app** on your phone or tablet.
2. Open the app and tap on the **Me** icon in the bottom right corner.
3. Tap on the **three dots** in the top right corner and select **Manage account**.
4. Tap on **Switch to Professional Account**.
5. Select **Business** as the account type.
6. Follow the prompts to complete the account setup process, including adding your business name, contact information, and any other required information.

Once your account is set up, you can start creating and sharing content to promote your Etsy shop. Keep in mind that TikTok may require you to verify your business account before you can access all the features and tools available to business accounts. This may involve providing additional information or documentation to prove that you are the owner of the business.

There are several ways you can use TikTok to promote your Etsy business:

Create and share posts about your products: Use TikTok's creative tools and features, such as music, effects, and filters, to create short, entertaining videos that highlight your products creatively and engagingly. Film clips of yourself sorting your supplies, making your items, using your products, and packing orders.

Participate in trends: TikTok is famous for trending dances, challenges, and filters. Participating in these is a fantastic way to create engagement. While the trends may not have anything to do with your business, because they are so popular, your posts are bound to get more views. Make sure to only participate in trends that are non-controversial and won't harm your business image.

Use relevant hashtags and tags: Just like with Twitter and Instagram, by including relevant hashtags and tags in your TikTok posts, you can make it easier for users to discover your content and interact with your account as well as hopefully visit your Etsy shop. The hashtags #etsy, #etsyshop, #maker, #crafter, #smallbusiness, and hashtags related to the products you sell can all help your content be found by other users.

As I mentioned in the Instagram section of this chapter, I keep a list of hashtags in the notes section of my phone that I just copy and paste into posts. TikTok allows you to write up to 2,200 characters in the caption of a post. However, it's worth noting that captions on TikTok are rarely read, as the main focus is on the video content and the related hashtags rather than the written text. A caption of around 100-200 characters is considered optimal for TikTok, as it allows for enough text to add context and engage with the audience, but still keeps the focus on the video. However, there are many times I only add hashtags with no other text.

Utilize TikTok's advertising features: TikTok's business accounts have access to advertising features that can help you reach a wider audience beyond those who follow your account and thus drive traffic to your Etsy shop. You can create and manage ads on TikTok to reach users who are interested in your products or related topics based on their activities on the app, which TikTok tracks. TikTok's advertising opportunities include:

- **In-feed ads:** These are native ads that appear in users' feeds, like sponsored posts on other social media platforms. They can be in the form of videos, photos, or carousels and can include a call-to-action button.
- **Brand takeover ads:** These are full-screen ads that appear when a user opens the app. They can be in the form of a video or image and are a great way to grab users' attention.
- **Branded hashtag challenge:** This feature allows businesses to create a hashtag challenge, which encourages users to create and share content using the designated hashtag.
- **Branded effects:** TikTok's AR effects allow businesses to create their own branded filters and lenses that users can use in their videos.
- **Branded hashtag stickers:** These are branded stickers that users can use in their videos and are associated with a specific hashtag.

To access TikTok's advertising platform, you will need to sign up for a **TikTok Ads** account. Here's how you can do that:

1. Go to the TikTok Ads website at **tiktok.com/business/ad-center**.
2. Click on the **Sign-Up** button in the top right corner of the page.
3. Fill in the required information to create a new account, including your name, email address, and password.

Once you have created your account, you can access TikTok's advertising platform by logging in to the TikTok Ads website and clicking on the **Create** button in the top right corner of the page. From there, you can choose the type of ad you want to create and follow the prompts to set up your campaign.

YouTube: Starting a YouTube channel can be a great way to promote your handmade products and thus drive traffic to your Etsy shop. While shoppers like photos, they love videos! And showcasing your products in videos so that users can examine your items from all angles and hear you talk about them can help turn watchers into buyers.

You don't even need a digital camera to film videos; I use my iPhone to film my YouTube videos. YouTube has over 2 billion active users and is the second-largest search engine in the world. By starting a channel, you can reach a larger audience and increase exposure for your products.

YouTube is a great platform to showcase your products through longer videos, unlike Instagram's and TikTok's shorter formats. You can apply the same ideas we discussed for Instagram Reels and TikTok clips to create engaging YouTube videos. Videos of you working on your products, discussing new releases, or giving updates on your Etsy shop's progress can attract viewers. Etsy is a popular home-based business topic on YouTube, and sharing your selling journey on the site can be interesting to many people.

However, while YouTube can help you grow your Etsy sales, be careful not to reveal all your trade secrets. Remember, your main goal is to make money. Some viewers may want to learn how to make your crafts and sell them themselves. While giving a glimpse into your creative process is fine, it's important to avoid providing step-by-step tutorials that create competition for your shop.

On the other hand, if you have crafting knowledge outside of the items you sell, you can consider sharing those methods on your YouTube channel. For instance, let's say you specialize in handmade Christmas stockings. But do you know how to make other, easier Christmas crafts that you're not interested in selling? Low-cost, simple how-to crafting videos are very popular on YouTube. Creating videos about easy-to-make Christmas ornaments, baking tutorials, or even showing various stocking stuffers you can buy at the dollar store to put in your custom stockings are all ideas that relate to your business but won't create competition for your shop. By sharing your knowledge on a broader range of crafts, you can attract more viewers to your channel and gain exposure for your Etsy shop without compromising your business.

Not sure how exactly YouTube works? Check out my book, *Beginner's Guide To Starting a YouTube Channel,* which is available on Amazon!

PRO TIP: An easy way to create multiple social media posts with one single clip is to film a 60-second TikTok video. Save that video and share it on Instagram as a Reel. The Reel will post to your Instagram static feed; from there, share the Reel to your Instagram Stories. If your Instagram and Facebook pages are linked, the clip will also post to your Facebook page. And if you have a YouTube channel, you can share the clip as a Short. One 60-second video will gain you maximum exposure across all of your social media platforms!

Etsy's Marketing Tools: While social media platforms such as Facebook, Instagram, Twitter, Pinterest, TikTok, and YouTube are all great ways to build your digital brand, Etsy itself offers several marketing tools to help sellers promote their products and reach new customers.

Some of the marketing tools available on Etsy include:

Shop Announcements: This feature allows you to create a message that will be displayed on your shop's homepage and in the emails you send to your customers. You can use this section to announce new product releases, highlight your best-selling products, share the story behind your shop, offer special promotions and discounts, and keep the customer informed of any changes or updates to your shop.

Etsy Ads: *Etsy Ads* allow you to create targeted ads that will be displayed to potential customers who are searching for products like yours on Etsy. To **create an ad for your shop on Etsy**, go to your **Seller Dashboard** and click on the **Marketing** tab. Click on **Etsy Ads**. Choose a daily budget anywhere from $1 to $100.

I recommend starting with $5 a day and letting the ad run for at least a week to see how it performs. If you are correctly utilizing Etsy SEO and are using social media to promote your shop, you may find that Etsy Ads aren't worth the added expense. I focus on SEO and social media to drive traffic to my shop. But the only way you can know for sure is to test Etsy Ads out for yourself.

Etsy Offsite Ads: As we've discussed, this feature allows you to place ads that will be displayed on other websites and platforms, such as Facebook, Instagram, Pinterest, and Google. For sellers with less than $10,000 in yearly sales, Etsy *Offsite Ads* are an optional program one needs to opt into. However, it is mandatory and automatic for shops that sell over $10,000 a year.

Remember that you only pay for an offsite ad if it leads to a sale. You do not pay if someone clicks on the ad but does not make a purchase. So, there is no risk to opting into these ads as you aren't going to lose money, but you will have the potential to make more.

You can end your *Offsite Ads* at any time unless you are automatically enrolled due to selling over $10,000 a year. There is no way to end or opt out of *Offsite Ads* for sellers who sell over $10,000. While this may seem unfair, to be honest, if you are selling over $10,000 a year on Etsy, *Offsite Ads* should be affordable for you. Again, you only pay if the click on an ad leads to a sale, meaning you aren't risking anything. Rather, you are making a sale when you otherwise wouldn't have made one.

To access the **Offside Ads** section of your account, go to your **Seller Dashboard** and click on the **Settings** tab. Then click on **Offsite Ads.**

Sales & Discounts: You can create various sales and discounts for both new and returning customers. You will find the **Sales & Discounts** section under the **Marketing** tab in your Etsy dashboard.

You can offer a **percentage off** the purchase price for a specific product or the entire order. For example, you could offer a 20% discount on all items within a certain shop section or a 20% discount on all orders over $50. Etsy automatically applies the discount for you, and the offer is shown under the thumbnail photos of your listings, which can help draw customers in.

For example, in my Etsy sticker shop, I may offer 30% off any three items. That 30% discount shows up under the price of all of my listings, which entices shoppers to click through to my shop to learn more about the sale. I find that when I run a sale, my orders increase, even if customers don't end up ordering enough to score the discount. The "On Sale" verbiage is enough to draw them in.

In contract to offering a percentage off, you can instead offer a **fixed amount off** the purchase price for a specific product or the entire order. For example, you could offer a $5 discount on all custom products in your shop or a $10 discount on orders over $100. I don't find this amount off option to be as effective as the percentage off option, but you should test it out to see which works best for your shop.

Sale events: Etsy allows sellers to create sales events, which allow you to offer a discount on a selection of your products for a limited time. Some of the offers you can send include:

- **Thank you:** Invite up to 200 recent customers back with a thank you offer by sending them an offer to show appreciation and encourage them to shop again. You can choose a discount amount of a percentage off or a fixed amount off.
- **Favorited item:** Turn favorites into orders by sending offers to anyone who favors one of your items. You can choose a discount percentage or a fixed amount off. Note that there is no minimum order option for the *favorited item* offers; it applies to the single item that someone has put into their cart.
- **Abandoned cart:** Remind shoppers to check out by sending an offer when someone leaves an item from your shop in their cart. As with *favorited items*, you can choose a discount percentage or a fixed amount off; and there is no minimum order amount as the offer applies to a single item that someone has put into their cart.
- **Run a sale:** Set lower prices for your whole shop or select categories. Many professional Etsy sellers will tell you that you should always be running sales and that your sales should be short-term for no longer than 48 hours. This is because Etsy will show shoppers a countdown clock of the remaining time in a sale, which can create a sense of urgency. These sellers typically run the same sale every two days. This can be hard to manage, however.

PRO TIP: Again, be careful with offering any discount or exclusive offer. The truth is that most Etsy sellers raise their prices over what the market rate is so that they can always have their items "on sale." And they often run short-term sales of 48 hours or less so that Etsy will show customers a count-down clock to encourage them to shop before the sale ends.

Is it frustrating to have to play this "sale" game to get orders? Yes. But it is a fact of the retail industry. People buy more items when they are on sale. Making sure you know your numbers so you can play the discount game to help you sell more items, not lose money.

Before offering any type of discount, I use an Etsy fee calculator to figure out my costs and actual net profit. There are many free Etsy fee calculators available online. My personal favorite is omniprofit.calculator.com/etsy-fee-calculator.

Create a promo code: Etsy allows shops to create a custom code to send to customers directly. You will need to enter a code name, a description of the offer, and the discount amount. You can also choose to set an expiration date and a minimum purchase amount. And you can manually end your coupon codes at any time.

Etsy does not distribute these coupon codes, however; that is something you need to do on your own. If you have a mailing list or Facebook group, you can share these special promo codes with those customers. I have a Facebook group specifically for my Etsy sticker shop and frequently create special promo codes just for members.

Blog/Website: Creating a blog or dedicated website can be a great way to establish your brand. However, it can also add more work to your plate. If you are only selling your crafts locally and on Etsy, you can use your Facebook business page as your "website." However, if you plan to expand your sales onto other platforms, a website might be something to consider.

Some things to consider when deciding whether to create a website include:

- Do you plan to author lengthy articles discussing the items you sell? Blogs are often seen as a research source on various topics. If you plan to only post new products and not offer any other information besides that, a website isn't worth your time as you can do the same for free on Facebook and the other social media platforms.

- Are you looking to use your site not just as a sales channel but also as a teaching tool? For example, if you are a quilter, do you want to expand into writing articles teaching people how to quilt or educating people about the history of quilting?
- Do you want to sell products only through Etsy or do you plan to eventually expand to selling on other platforms? If you do want to eventually grow beyond Etsy, then a website could serve as a landing page for all of your links. And many web hosting services also offer the ability to add a store right on your website.
- Do you want to explore affiliate advertising or sell advertising on your site to earn extra money? Google AdSense and Amazon Associates are just two of the programs that allow you to earn money by placing links on your blog.

If you answered "yes" to any of the above questions, then you may want to consider starting a website. However, you will need to decide whether to go with a free blogging platform or a paid website. If you decide to go the paid route, you can invest in a sophisticated system or choose a simple, low-cost one.

Yes, there are lots of decisions to make when deciding whether or not to start a website!

You can create a blog for your Etsy shop using several free platforms, such as Blogger and WordPress. It's worth noting that Google owns Blogger, which means you can apply for a Google AdSense account and place ads on your blog to generate extra revenue. A blog can be a useful tool to monetize your online presence, drive traffic to your Etsy listings, and increase sales.

If you decide to create a paid website for your Etsy shop, remember that your Etsy shop should remain the focus of your brand, with your blog or website serving as an additional tool to drive traffic to your listings. There are many low-cost website options available, such as GoDaddy.com and Wix.com, which offer not only URL registrations but also inexpensive hosting and simple website-building tools. And they also offer the ability to, for a price, sell your products directly on their sites.

Because I use the pen name *Jean Lee* for both my Etsy shop and the stationery products I sell on Amazon, I have a website at JeanLeePublishing.com that I pay for through GoDaddy that serves as a landing page for both platforms. When you register a URL with GoDaddy, they will offer you add-on options such as a website. This is the option I use for my *Jean Lee* site as it is inexpensive and easy to maintain. I can easily tell people my site is at "Jean Lee Publishing dot com." From there, they can choose to click through to my Amazon Author Page or my Etsy Shop.

Domain Name: Whether you look at your handmade crafts as a side hustle or a full-time business, you want to secure the domain name for your company. A domain name is a personal website address closely tied to your Etsy shop name. This can make it easier for customers to find and remember your website, as well as give you a professional online presence. I own several domain names for my various businesses; I make sure to always lock in a name whenever I start a new venture to ensure that I own the URLs before someone else snatches them up.

You can purchase domain names through websites like **GoDaddy.com** and link them to your Etsy shop and other online platforms. For example, I have the domain **AnnEckhart.com** that directs users directly to my Amazon Storefront where all my books are listed. And **JeanLeePublishing.com** takes users to a website that directs them to my Etsy shop or my Amazon page for my stationery brand, both of which I have under the same pen name.

When thinking about registering for a domain name, it's important to consider where you want the URL to direct users. Do you want people to go to your website first, or do you want them to always go directly to your Etsy shop? It's important to remember that a site should *complement* your Etsy shop, rather than serve as a replacement for it. So, unless you are selling products on multiple websites the way I am, you want your URL to point to Etsy.

If you are using a free blog on a platform like Blogger, you may want to choose a domain name that directs people directly to your Etsy shop, such as "MyStore.com", and keep the URL provided by Blogger for your blog as-is. Or you could choose a different domain name specifically for your blog, such as "MyEtsyShopBlog.com".

In my opinion, if you are only selling on Etsy, it's important to have a personalized URL address that points directly to your Etsy shop, as your primary focus should always be on driving sales through Etsy. A website should work to direct traffic to your Etsy listings, rather than intercept it. But if Etsy is your only online selling platform, you can easily use a Facebook business page as a sort of website as you can put multiple links there, which will save you time and money over building a stand-alone site. And in the future, if you do grow beyond Etsy, you can easily start a website then and redirect the URL to your site then.

Mailing List: Creating a loyal customer base for your crafts means you will have repeat customers who come back to your Etsy shop again and again because they love your products. And if you are utilizing social media, your customers may have gotten to know you on a more personal level, which also leads to strong customer loyalty. Shoppers are impressed by brands that get to know their customers, and if you engage with your following on social media, that engagement will translate to repeat buyers.

And while social media is a great way to reach customers, to keep your most loyal buyers informed and engaged, you may want to consider setting up a mailing list that you can use to send out newsletters. Mailing lists and newsletters offer an affordable way for you to connect directly with buyers by offering giveaways, special discount codes, and a first look at new products.

Most mailing services have free options that allow you to start collecting and growing your email lists, allowing you to upgrade to paid versions once you have reached a larger following. Some popular mailing list services include:

- AWeber
- Campaign Monitor
- Constant Contact
- Drip
- GetResponse
- Mailchimp

These services provide tools for creating and managing email campaigns, including email design templates, subscriber lists, analytics, and automation features. Many also offer integrations with other marketing and sales tools, such as e-commerce platforms and CRM software. You can create a landing page to collect email addresses; and if you sell your crafts locally, you can collect email addresses using a sign-up sheet in your vendor booth.

PRO TIP: If you do start to collect email addresses for a mailing list, make sure you keep a file of those addresses on your computer system or backup hard drive, not only on the mailing list server. If you decide to stop using that mailing service, you will lose access to those emails. Always make sure you have a backup so you can start a new list with another service if you decide to.

Note that many blogs and website platforms also have a built-in mailing list feature. For example, my site JeanLeePublishing.com, which is through GoDaddy, has a feature where visitors can enter their email addresses to join my mailing list. I can use GoDaddy's newsletter feature or transfer the email addresses to another platform.

Remember to only send emails to individuals who have specifically opted in to receive them so that you comply with anti-spam laws and avoid annoying or alienating your customers. Send newsletters sparingly, no more than once a week. And only send newsletters when you have interesting and valuable content to share. It's better to send a monthly newsletter that is jam-packed with good content than it is to send weekly newsletters with little value.

Putting It All Together: If you're feeling overwhelmed by all the different social networking sites, marketing techniques, and advertising possibilities, take a deep breath and remember to take things one step at a time. Start with Facebook, as it is the easiest and most effective. Then expand to Twitter, Pinterest, and Instagram, as you can stick to static posts on all of them. If you feel comfortable adding videos, you can expand to TikTok and YouTube. Or just choose one site to focus on, the one you most enjoy. Some Etsy shops only use Facebook, while others use TikTok exclusively.

When you have an Etsy shop, your primary focus should be creating new products and getting those items listed. Hopefully, you'll stay busy processing orders, too. Etsy SEO along with good photos are essential in creating an Etsy listing that will result in shoppers finding your products. Think of social media as a bonus step in the listing creation process.

To promote your listings on social media, remember that you can use the "share" buttons provided by Etsy in every active listing. Simply click on the buttons for Facebook, Twitter, and Pinterest to share your listings on these platforms. As we've discussed, hashtags are incredibly useful to increase the visibility of your social media posts on Twitter, Instagram, and TikTok. Once you have connected your Etsy account to your social media networks, you can easily share your listings with just a few clicks and add a handful of relevant hashtags.

To avoid overwhelming your followers on Facebook with multiple listings at once, I recommend spreading your posts out. You can schedule posts on Facebook to space them out over the day. On Twitter and Pinterest, it is generally okay to share posts one after the other as the feeds on both platforms move much faster than on Facebook.

To promote your business on Instagram, it is important to post regularly and engage with other users. Try to post at least once a day You can share photos of your office, new inventory, or even personal moments to give your followers a behind-the-scenes look at your business. Don't forget to include three to five hashtags with each post to make it easier for potential customers to find you. Try adding videos to Instagram through Reels and Stories. Once you are comfortable creating videos, consider expanding to TikTok and even YouTube. You can add 60-second videos to YouTube as a Short.

If you have the time and resources to create and maintain a website, it can be a great way to promote your handmade wares. However, remember that a website will require additional work and resources, so it's important to make sure it is worth the investment. I don't recommend a website unless you expand to selling on sites other than Etsy. A mailing list requires less work and may be more effective than a website, so consider adding that option before anything else.

Always remember that your number one goal with your business is to make money. Your priority should always be developing new products, creating new listings, and maximizing Etsy SEO. You may find that you do enough on Etsy alone to make sales and that you don't even need social media. But if you do need a boost, then social media platforms are an easy, effective, and free way to advertise.

CHAPTER SEVEN: ETSY ACCOUNTING MADE EASY

DISCLAIMER: This chapter is for informational purposes only. You should always consult with a certified public accountant (CPA) to discuss the tax laws that apply to your business. Every state and country is different when it comes to taxes, so be sure to consult with a tax professional in your area for advice on how to manage your own Etsy bookkeeping.

Let's be honest: Making money is fun, but dealing with taxes and bookkeeping is not. However, when you're running your own business, keeping track of your finances is an essential part of your operations. You have to know your numbers to make sure you're turning a profit, and you must report your earnings to the government come tax time.

And when you sell online, there is no way to "hide" money. There is an electronic record of how much money Etsy pays you, and Etsy will also issue you a 1099 form at the end of the year for you to file taxes. To reduce your tax bill, you need to track your business expenses. It's easy to keep a record of your sales as Etsy does it for you, but you will need to record your deductions on your own.

Etsy provides sellers with a lot of financial information to help them keep track of shop numbers. Specifically, Etsy breaks down seller expenses, including the fees paid to them and the cost of any ads or promotions. Etsy automatically deducts these expenses from each seller's account and deposits the remaining funds into each seller's bank account.

Every business has different expenses that come with it. With a craft business, there are numerous expenses that you will need to track to maximize your deductions come tax time. So while Etsy automatically deducts their selling fees, advertising fees, and shipping costs from your balance, you still have to keep track of additional expenses on your end.

Before we discuss how to track your business expenses, let's first cover the financial information Etsy provides all sellers. You can find these details updated in real-time in your account. From your **Shop Manager** dashboard, click on **Finances** to access the following:

Payment Account: The *Payment Account* section is where you can manage your payment and deposit information. To receive payment for the items you sell, you must link your bank account to Etsy. You have the option to choose your preferred deposit schedule from daily, weekly, every other week, or monthly transfers. I choose weekly payouts so that I can count on a weekly "paycheck." But if you are doing a large volume of orders and are having to frequently purchase supplies, you may opt for daily payouts to cover those expenses.

Monthly Statements: The *Monthly Statements* section is, in my opinion, the most important part of the *Finances* area. Here you can access information about your sales, fees, marketing expenses, shipping costs, and net profit. You can view your monthly statements dating back to the beginning of your selling account or narrow down the time frame to however you choose. I

Regularly monitoring your net profit will give you an idea of whether you are making money or incurring a loss. Remember, though, to keep in mind that the net profit displayed by Etsy does not include your offline expenses, such as your internet costs, cell phone fees, craft supplies, and shipping materials. I like to track my monthly profits from year to year to see which months I can expect more sales and to also see if my sales are growing.

QuickBooks for Etsy: For a fee, you can sync your Etsy seller account with *Intuit QuickBooks* to track your sales, expenses, and tax deductions.

TurboTax for Etsy: For a fee, you can sync your Etsy seller account with *TurboTax*, which will organize your account for taxes.

Legal & Tax Information: The *Legal & Tax Information* section is where you will enter all the necessary legal information for your Etsy shop. It is in this section that you will be able to download your 1099 form at the end of the year, which is required for tax filing purposes. If you sell more than $600 within the year, Etsy will generate a 1099 tax form for you. Note that even if you are not issued a tax form, you still must report all income to the IRS.

Fees: All selling platforms charge their sellers fees, and Etsy is no exception. As we've already discussed, the fees Etsy charges cover the costs of operating the platform and providing services to its users. These fees include a **listing fee**, a **transaction fee**, and a **payment processing fee.**

To recap from earlier in this book, Etsy charges a **listing fee** whenever a seller creates a new listing. This fee is currently $0.20 per listing and is charged at the time the listing is created. Listings are active for four months and can be renewed by the seller at the end of that period for an additional $0.20. That means you can list one item for a year for only $.80.

Etsy also charges a **transaction fee** whenever an item sells. This fee is currently 5% of the item's sale price, plus any shipping and gift wrap charges. The transaction fee is charged at the time the sale is made.

Finally, Etsy charges a **payment processing fee** whenever they process a sale. This fee varies depending on the payment method used but is typically around 3% of the total transaction amount plus a fixed fee.

The payment processing fee is deducted from the seller's account at the time the payment is processed.

Expenses: All businesses can claim business-related expenses as deductions on their taxes. With an Etsy craft shop, your expenses will include:

- **Fees:** The fees charged by Etsy are automatically deducted from your account before your net profit is disbursed to you. If the fees are not specified on the tax form issued by Etsy, then you shouldn't need to report them during tax season. However, check with your CPA or tax preparer to be sure you are following the current tax laws for your area.
- **Craft Supplies:** The biggest expense for makers are the supplies needed to make their wares. If you have already been selling your handmade products locally, you may already have a system in place for tracking these costs. I use a credit card with a good points rewards system to purchase all supplies for my business. This makes my costs easy to track. If you buy all of your crafting supplies from two or three locations and charge those purchases to one credit card or business debit card, you will be able to account for those charges easily every month.
- **Office Supplies:** Pens, paper, paperclips, printer ink, and any other office supplies you use to run your Etsy shop can all be claimed as business expenses.
- **Shipping Supplies:** Next to craft supplies, shipping supplies are usually the next biggest expense for Etsy craft shops. Shipping boxes, tape, shipping labels, and packing materials can all add up quickly. Just as I charge my supplies to a credit card, I also charge my shipping supplies. I only order shipping supplies from three different companies, which makes keeping track of those expenses easy.

- **Advertising & Marketing:** Etsy will automatically deduct any charges for their ads, whether they are regular ads or off-site ads. However, if you advertise on Facebook or other social media websites, you will need to track those expenses yourself. You can see your yearly Facebook ad expenses in your Facebook account. If you order extra products for giveaways or collaborations, you should be able to claim those costs under marketing.
- **Home Office:** If you run your Etsy business from home, you may be able to claim a portion of your rent, utilities, and other home office expenses as a tax deduction.
- **Communications:** You can claim your internet service for your Etsy business. And if you use your smartphone for any business-related tasks, you can claim that as well.
- **Business Travel:** If you attend craft shows or other events related to your business, you can claim the cost of transportation, lodging, and meals as a deduction.
- **Legal & Professional Fees:** This includes the cost of any legal or professional services you use in connection with your Etsy shop, such as accounting or tax preparation services.
- **Website Services:** If you pay for a dedicated URL, standalone website, and/or a mailing list service, you can claim them as business expenses.

Tracking your Etsy business expenses: There are several ways you can track your Etsy expenses to help manage your business and prepare for tax time. Here are a few options you can consider:

- **Use Etsy's built-in invoicing and payment tools to track your income and expenses.** These tools can help you keep track of the money you have earned, the fees you have paid to Etsy, and the expenses you have incurred in running your business.

- **Use accounting software to manage your finances.** There are many different accounting software options available, and some are specifically designed for small businesses or online marketplaces like Etsy. These tools track your income and expenses, generate reports, and prepare for tax time. TurboTax is the most popular of these services.
- **Keep detailed records of your income and expenses, such as receipts, invoices, and bank statements on a computer spreadsheet or even in a notebook.** Most of your income and expenses will be recorded online on Etsy and your credit card and bank statements. This makes transferring that data to your computer or paper easy.
- **Hire a certified public accountant or professional tax preparer**. Turning to an expert to handle your financial management and tax preparation can be money well spent. In addition to filing your taxes, they can also provide expert guidance on managing your finances.

My Way: Etsy automatically deducts fees and advertising costs from my account and only pays me the remaining balance, which is displayed under **Net Profit** in my Etsy account. At the end of the year, Etsy provides me with a 1099 form that lists my net profit after all of their fees have been deducted. On my end, I only need to keep track of my deductions that occur outside of the platform, meaning I do not need to track my Etsy fees or Etsy advertising expenses.

Remember that your gross sales are your sales BEFORE any fees or expenses are taken out. On Etsy, they will show you your NET profit after they take THEIR fees and advertising costs. However, as noted earlier, there are many more expenses you can claim as deductions when it comes time to file your taxes.

I use a basic spreadsheet to track my monthly expenses. Every month I record what I paid for web services (GoDaddy and MailChimp), advertising costs (Facebook and TikTok ads), communications expenses (internet and cell phone), inventory, office supplies, and shipping supplies. I also use an app to track my mileage.

Those are my only month-to-month business expenses. My accountant figures out how much I can claim for my home office, and he also figures out how much mileage I can claim along with any travel costs I may have had that year.

At the end of the year, I tally every category of expenses to get the year-end total for each. For example, I will add up my internet and cell phone charges for each month and enter that number into my year-end communications field. Even though I have a CPA who files my taxes for me, I still provide him with these expense breakdowns so he can accurately file my returns.

At the end of January, I download my 1099 form from Etsy. I take that along with my list of year-end expenses to my accountant so he can file my taxes. Easy!

CHAPTER EIGHT: CUSTOMER SERVICE

If you have experience selling your crafts locally, then you hopefully have some good customer service experience under your belt. While local vendor fairs tend to be drama free in terms of customer issues, selling online can be different. Online, people can hide behind screen names, which makes some people think they can say whatever they want to sellers. And while the vast majority of Etsy customers are wonderful people, now and then, a difficult customer will come along that will make you question why you started your business in the first place!

The best way to deal with customer service issues is to avoid them in the first place. Having clear policies stated in your listings and in your shop will help protect you in case a customer makes a claim against you. For example, if a customer claims that they wanted their order customized, but you didn't have customization set up in the listing, then Etsy will back you if the customer files a claim.

It's not enough to just state your policies, though; you need to live up to them on your end. Here are some ways you can stay on top of customer service to avoid problems:

Set realistic shipping times: It's important to be upfront with customers about how long it will take for their order to be shipped. If you only create a product when an order comes in, it will take you longer to fulfill that order compared to if you have several items already made. Consider factors like production time, packaging, and shipping carrier turnaround times when determining shipping estimates.

I like to set a longer processing time than I need. I may enter a processing time of three days but usually ship most orders the following business day. When you first start selling on Etsy, I wouldn't list any items that aren't already made. You don't want to list that you have 10 hand-knitted baby caps ready if you haven't started making even one. Or that you have 1000 vanilla soy candles available for purchase if you are still waiting on a wax delivery. Only listing the inventory you have in stock and shipping it out faster than promised will go a long way toward avoiding problems.

If you offer customization, you can make products ahead and add personalization when an order comes in, which will make your process faster. Most customers understand that custom orders take sellers longer to complete. Look at other shops that offer customization and not how long their handling times are.

Managing customer expectations: When a customer places an Etsy order from your shop unless you are shipping the item immediately, you may want to send them a message letting them know when their order will be shipped, and what to expect in terms of shipping times. If there are any delays or unexpected issues, let the customer know as soon as possible. While you should have your handling time clearly stated, and while Etsy will show the customer how long it will take for their item to arrive once you've shipped it, it never hurts to send your customer a quick note to reassure them that you are working on their order and when to expect it.

If you are selling customizable products, then you want to message your customer before you start working on their order to confirm the details. While they should fill out this information during the checkout process, it never hurts to double-check to ensure they entered the information correctly. Nothing is worse than starting a custom order just to get a message that the buyer made a mistake.

Handling lost or damaged shipments: Unfortunately, packages can sometimes be lost or damaged in transit. I have been selling online since 2005 on all of the major platforms, and the vast majority of packages arrived with no issues. However, when a package has been lost or arrives at the customer's location, damaged, it's important to immediately address the situation.

When a customer contacts you to report that their package has not arrived, the first step is to check the tracking information. If the tracking information shows that the item was delivered, it is best to ask the customer to wait for a couple of days. Sometimes, packages are delivered to a neighbor's house, or they may have been scanned as delivered but still be on the mail truck. Often, it turns out that someone else in the household has brought the delivery inside but didn't tell the actual customer about the package. I always encourage my buyers to wait for a few days to see if their package turns up. I usually do.

However, if a buyer's package still hasn't arrived after a couple of days, kindly direct your customer to contact their local Post Office or speak to their mail carrier. Explain that the package is now in the hands of the USPS in their area and that you have no control over it once it leaves your hands. It's important to maintain a professional and helpful attitude, as the customer will likely be frustrated. By providing them with clear guidance, you empower them to act.

If there is no resolution from the Post Office, you then need to direct your customer to file a claim with Etsy. Since you shipped the label through Etsy and the tracking information shows it as delivered, Etsy will take responsibility for the missing package and refund the customer, without any financial loss on your part. This is part of Etsy's protection program for both buyers and sellers, which is one of the many benefits of selling on Etsy.

If a package arrives to your customer with visible damage to the shipping box, you may be able to put in a claim with USPS, but only if you shipped the item via Priority Mail, as Priority comes with up to $50 in insurance. However, it may be easier for you to refund the customer directly and then seek a refund directly from the Post Office as asking the customer to file a claim can often be confusing and time-consuming. Note that you will need photographic evidence of the damaged box to file a claim.

If an order arrives with the product inside damaged, but there is no damage to the shipping box, it may be harder to prove that it was the Post Office's fault, and filing a claim with USPS may not be successful. In this case, you may need to absorb the cost of the refund. If an item arrives damaged, I issue the buyer a refund and tell them to keep the item. Asking the customer to return the damaged product is an inconvenience to them. And as a seller, having the item shipped back to you means that in addition to issuing a refund for the original order, you then have to pay for the return postage. It's easier and cheaper to just issue a full refund and allow the customer to keep the product, which they can repair, donate, or throw away.

To avoid products breaking during shipment, it's essential to overpack orders to ensure the item has the best chance of arriving intact. If you are getting multiple reports of products breaking during shipment, it's a lesson that you need to do a better job packing your orders. Bubble wrap and packing peanuts are essential for shipping breakables. After I package an order, I shake the box. If I hear or feel anything moving around inside the package, I open it back up and add more packing materials.

Responding to messages on Etsy: While selling online means you often have little to no direct interaction with customers, you will on occasion get messages through Etsy regarding your products and orders. It's important to respond to these messages as quickly as possible as Etsy rates your response time. If you are slow to answer messages, it will reflect poorly on your shop. I have the Etsy app installed on my phone so that I can respond to messages quickly no matter where I am, even if it is just to tell the person messaging me that I am away from the office but will answer their question when I get back.

Every seller eventually has a customer message them upset that their order hasn't arrived, they were sent the wrong item, or that the product was damaged during shipment. While it can be difficult to deal with an upset buyer, it's important to remain calm and professional. When a customer is angry, try to respond with empathy and understanding. For example, you might say, "I'm sorry to hear that there's an issue with your order. Let me see what I can do to help."

If the customer claims that an item arrived damaged, ask them to send photos of the product. Almost everyone has a smartphone, which makes it easy for the buyer to take a photo and sent it to you through Etsy's messaging system. If the photos confirm that the item was damaged during shipping, apologize, and offer a full refund.

In cases where the mistake was the buyer's fault, such as entering the wrong shipping address or making an error when ordering, it's important to explain politely but firmly that you are unable to refund the purchase due to your shop policies and the fact that the mistake wasn't your fault. If the customers persist, encourage them to file a claim with Etsy. Etsy should side with you and decline the return.

Only use Etsy's messaging system: I do not give out my email or phone number to customers as I want to make sure all communications go through Etsy. Etsy can access messages, so if you are being harassed or threatened by an upset customer, you will have the messages as evidence. However, if the communication happens outside of Etsy, you lose your *Seller Protection.*

Managing customer expectations: As I've mentioned previously, I like to "under promise and over deliver" when it comes to my online shops. While I usually ship orders the following business day, I set my handling times for two to three days to give me a buffer. If I can ship earlier, the customer is happy. I also, when possible, upgrade shipping. While I may list an item with Parcel as the shipping method, I usually upgrade the order to ship via Priority Mail. Not only is Priority faster, but I can also use a free USPS box.

Don't oversell: I also make sure to not oversell my products, meaning I don't make claims that simply aren't true. I state the facts of the product, such as the size and materials. I make sure to disclose any potential issues a customer may face, such as care and washing instructions. I take crisp, clear photos to ensure the products I'm selling are shown as-is. And I work to offer fair pricing and shipping charges.

I don't claim any of the items I sell will change someone's life or that they are the best products of their kind on the market. While national name brands may be able to make such bold claims, I, as a small business owner, cannot. I don't promise same-day shipping when I know I will need a day or two to process a sale.

Dealing with difficult buyers: Sometimes, despite your best efforts, you simply cannot make a buyer happy resulting in them leaving you negative feedback. In these cases, it's important to remain calm and professional and to remember that negative feedback is not always a reflection of the quality of your products or your customer service. As your business grows, it is easier to absorb one or two bad reviews along the way as your positive feedback will eventually cancel out the negative.

However, when you are selling handmade items that you have put your heart into creating, a negative response from a buyer can really hurt. Remember that when dealing with a difficult buyer, it's important to listen carefully to their concerns and try to understand their perspective. Even if you disagree with their complaints, showing empathy and understanding can go a long way toward defusing a tense situation. Many buyers have had negative experiences dealing with online sellers and come out swinging. Gently let them know you hear their concerns and are going to help them, which should calm them down.

But if you can't calm down a customer and they escalate to threatening you, you must take action to protect yourself and your shop. Here are some steps you can take to get Etsy to intervene:

1. **Contact Etsy:** You can report the buyer to Etsy by clicking on the "Contact Etsy Support" link on the Etsy homepage. You can also contact Etsy through the "Help" section of your shop dashboard.
2. **Provide evidence:** When reporting the buyer, be sure to provide evidence of their threatening behavior, such as screenshots of their messages or any other communication you have had with them.
3. **Flag the conversation:** You can also flag the conversation with the buyer as inappropriate or abusive. This will alert Etsy to the situation and may lead to the buyer's account being suspended or banned.

Etsy takes reports of threatening or abusive behavior very seriously and has policies in place to protect sellers from harassment. Don't escalate a bad situation by continuing to engage with an abusive buyer. By taking action and reporting the buyer's behavior to Etsy directly, you can help protect both yourself and your business.

Dealing with negative feedback: In situations where the buyer leaves negative feedback, it's important to remain calm. If the customer never reached out to you regarding their order, you can contact them through Etsy, let them know you saw their feedback, and apologize for any issues they experienced. You can then offer a solution, such as a full refund or a replacement product, on the condition that they retract their feedback. Sometimes buyers forget that there is a real person on the other end of the computer and don't consider contacting a seller with a problem.

Remember that dealing with difficult buyers is a part of running a business and that it's impossible to please everyone all of the time. I don't know of any Etsy seller who has never gotten negative feedback. It happens. Try to move past it and focus on the other orders you have to process. Eventually, the one negative feedback will be buried by the positive ones you get.

Issuing refunds: If you made a mistake with an order, you need to take responsibility for it and refund the customer immediately. I prefer to issue a refund and allow the buyer to keep the item. My error has already caused a problem for my customer; I don't want to make them take the time to repackage and ship me back the defective product, especially since I have to pay for the return postage.

Here's a step-by-step guide on how to issue a refund to a customer on Etsy:

1. Go to your Etsy shop dashboard
2. Click on **Orders & Shipping**
3. Find the order
4. Click on **Issue a refund**
5. Choose the refund amount
6. Choose the reason for the refund
7. Add a message to the buyer (optional)
8. Click **Review refund**
9. Click **Issue refund**

Once you have issued the refund, Etsy will process the refund and notify the buyer. The refund will typically be issued back to the original payment method used by the buyer. It is important to note that Etsy may withhold payment for the refunded amount from your shop payment account, depending on your payment processing settings and the timing of the refund.

You not only have to refund the cost of the item but the shipping, too. Depending on the issue, Etsy may or may not refund you the fees from the sale.

Etsy Seller Protection: Selling on Etsy automatically enrolls you in their *Seller Protection* program, which is designed to help protect sellers on the platform from certain types of fraudulent activities, including payment disputes, cases of unauthorized transactions, and claims of non-delivery of items. The policy includes the following measures:

1. **Payment protection:** Etsy provides payment protection for sellers who use *Etsy Payments* to process their transactions. This means that if a buyer files a payment dispute, Etsy will investigate and work to resolve the issue, and will cover any eligible losses incurred by the seller up to the full value of the transaction.

2. **Seller protection cases:** If a buyer opens a case against a seller for non-delivery, the seller can provide proof of shipment or delivery to dispute the claim. If the seller can provide proof, the case will be closed in the seller's favor, and the seller will not be responsible for refunding the buyer.

3. **Seller protection for unauthorized transactions:** If a seller receives an unauthorized transaction, Etsy will investigate and work to resolve the issue, and will cover any eligible losses incurred by the seller up to the full value of the transaction.

Contacting Etsy Seller Support: As an Etsy seller, there are several ways to reach out to Etsy for help:

1. **Contact Etsy's customer support team:** You can contact Etsy's customer support team by visiting the **Etsy Help Center**, which is located at the bottom of every Etsy page, and clicking on the **Contact support** button. From there, you can choose the topic that best matches your issue and fill out a support request form. Etsy's support team will then respond to your request via email.

2. **Use Etsy's Seller Help Center:** Etsy's *Seller Help Center* is a comprehensive resource that provides answers to many common questions and issues that sellers may encounter. You can browse the help center's articles and guides to find information on topics such as setting up your shop, managing your orders, and resolving disputes.

3. **Join the Etsy Community:** The *Etsy Community* is a forum where sellers can connect with each other and share advice and support. You can ask questions and get advice from other sellers who may have experienced similar issues or challenges. Or you can just lurk and pick up information without posting yourself.

4. **Follow Etsy's social media channels:** Etsy frequently shares updates and announcements on its social media channels, including Twitter, Facebook, and Instagram. Following their profiles on social media can help you stay up-to-date on changes to Etsy's policies and procedures, as well as any issues or outages that may affect your shop.

PRO TIP: If, for some reason, you aren't getting a response from Etsy through their website, you can message them through social media, specifically Facebook. This will get you talking to a live person who may be able to help you faster.

Regardless of how you choose to reach out to Etsy for help, it's important to be professional and specific about your issue or question. Make sure you provide any relevant details or documentation to support your request. Etsy's customer support team is generally very responsive and helpful, so don't hesitate to reach out if you need assistance. Treat the team with the respect you hope that customers treat you and refrain from badgering or threats, both of which could result in your account being terminated.

Etsy Buyer Protection: Just as sellers are offered protection in certain circumstances, so are Etsy buyers. As a seller, you must understand these policies just so that you know where your customers would stand in case an issue arises. Etsy offers several buyer protections to help ensure that buyers have a positive experience when shopping on the platform. Some of these protections include:

1. **Buyer Protection Case:** If a buyer has an issue with an order, they can open a *Buyer Protection Case* within the designated timeframe to seek resolution with the seller. The buyer protection case is designed to help buyers and sellers work together to resolve issues such as non-delivery, damaged items, or items that do not match the description provided by the seller.

2. **Refund Policy:** Etsy's refund policy requires sellers to accept returns and issue refunds for items that are not as described, defective, or arrive damaged, regardless of whether or not their shop policies accept returns. Buyers have 180 days to file a refund request from the date of the purchase.

3. **Etsy's Payment Processing System:** Etsy's payment processing system provides additional protection for buyers by keeping their payment information secure and encrypted. Buyers can use various payment methods, including credit cards, debit cards, and PayPal, to make purchases on the

platform. Sellers never see what payment a customer uses as Etsy handles all payments themselves.

4. **Reviews & Ratings:** Etsy's review system allows buyers to leave feedback on their purchases, including ratings and reviews of the product and the seller. This helps other buyers make informed decisions and encourages sellers to maintain high standards of quality and customer service. The ability for customers to leave public feedback is one more reason why you want to try and avoid issues in the first place.

Contacting Etsy Buyer Support: As a buyer on Etsy, there are several ways to reach out to Etsy for help:

1. **Contact Etsy's customer support team:** Customers can contact Etsy's customer support team by visiting the **Etsy Help Center** and clicking on the **Contact support** button. From there, they can choose the topic that best matches their issue and fill out a support request form. Etsy's support team will then respond via email.

2. **Use Etsy's Buyer Help Center:** Etsy's *Buyer Help Center* is a comprehensive resource that provides answers to many common questions and issues that buyers may encounter. Shoppers can browse the help center's articles and guides to find information on topics such as making purchases, tracking orders, and resolving disputes.

3. **Reach out to the seller:** If a customer has an issue with an order, their first step is typically to reach out to the seller directly to try to resolve the issue. Buyers can do this by clicking on the Contact option in their order history.

When I talk to people about my online selling journey and dealing with customer service issues, I always joke that 99.9% of buyers are amazing. It's the .1% who make things difficult. However, I do my best to prevent customer complaints from happening by making sure my listings and policies are clear and that I ship orders quickly. I answer messages within an hour of them coming in. And I work hard to make things right when I make a mistake. "Under promise and over deliver" and you, too, can prevent most Etsy customer service issues from occurring in the first place.

The *Golden Rule* applies in life and business: Treat others the way you want to be treated. And that includes dealing with your Etsy buyers.

CHAPTER NINE: GROWING YOUR BUSINESS

Hopefully, this book has given you all of the tools and resources you need to start selling your handmade wares on Etsy. Numerous makers only sell on Etsy, and there are others who also still sell at local craft fairs.

But other crafters have expanded their online selling beyond Etsy. And that's what we will cover in this chapter.

First, however, I want to reiterate the fact that choosing to only sell your crafts on Etsy is perfectly fine. Expanding to other websites takes time. Not only time to learn each platform, but time to create new products and list them. Etsy is the number one e-commerce site for crafters to sell their goods. If you decide to stick with Etsy, you aren't failing in any way. In fact, for many sellers, focusing on their Etsy shop is the smartest way to grow their business.

However, if you do want to expand to other online platforms, you have options. First, let's break down the pros and cons of expanding your business beyond Etsy:

PROS:

1. **Increased revenue:** Selling on more platforms means that you will reach more customers and potentially make more money. While Etsy has a large customer base, other websites get a lot more traffic, including Amazon and eBay, the number one and number three selling platforms in America.
2. **Diversification:** Selling on multiple platforms can help diversify your income streams and reduce your reliance on one platform. If you inadvertently (or deliberately) violate

Etsy's rules, you could lose your account. Having accounts on other sites would mean you have backup places to sell. Of course, there are many things you can do to prevent this, but if you are a full-time crafter, having backup platforms is comforting "just in case."

3. **Branding:** Creating your own online store or selling on multiple platforms can help you build a more recognizable brand and increase your visibility. Think of all of the big brands that are sold at multiple stores. Hallmark has their own stores, but you can also find Hallmark products at Walmart, Target, Walgreens, CVS, and other national retailers, which has allowed them to build its brand beyond its own locations. Hallmark no longer relies on customers having access to a Hallmark store to buy Hallmark products.

4. **Customization:** Having your own online shop or selling on other platforms can give you more control over the design and customization of your store. While Etsy does offer options for personalizing the look of your shop, you are limited in what you can do. A brand such as Happy Planners has a very unique color pallet that they can maximize by selling on their own platform versus relying on other websites.

5. **Experimentation:** If you have built an Etsy shop based around one category, selling on other platforms can allow you to expand your offerings. Note that you can also accomplish this by opening up a second Etsy shop, which we will discuss shortly. Etsy's algorithm likes shops to have very specific niches, which makes adding new products difficult. But other websites don't have the same SEO structure as Etsy, making it easier to flesh out your brand to multiple products under one site.

CONS:

1. **Learning curve:** Selling on multiple platforms may require you to learn new systems and processes, which can be time-consuming and challenging. Every platform has its own listing forms, payment processing system, and shipping options. Managing Etsy alone is a lot; managing several others may be too much, especially when you are handmaking every product you sell. You want to spend the majority of your time creating products, not struggling to manage several websites.

2. **Higher fees:** Some platforms may charge higher fees than Etsy, which can impact your profits. If you are selling products with low-profit margins, listing on other websites may not make sense financially as the fees will be more than your net income. You will likely have to spend more time driving traffic to these other platforms, too; and time is money.

3. **Increased workload:** Expanding your business beyond Etsy may require you to handle more orders, which may become too overwhelming for you to fulfill on your own. You may need to hire help to run your business, which will cut into your profits. And having help means you will have to trust those people to meet your standards. And let's face it: When it comes to handmaking products, no one else will ever meet your standards of quality.

4. **More marketing:** Etsy SEO allows sellers to maximize the visibility of their listings both on Etsy and off. If you expand to other websites, you will have to increase your social media marketing efforts. And the more you spend on marketing, the less time you have to create products. While other sites may have more traffic, they may not have as many handmade

shoppers, making it more challenging to bring in buyers for your products.

5. **Expansion stress:** Growing your business will likely require you to expand your workspace and hire employees. Renting office space and dealing with payroll may be more stressful than you want to take on. If you are busy enough selling your crafts locally and on Etsy, and if you want to stay a one-person operation, expanding to other platforms may not be feasible.

Opening a Second Etsy Shop: As you can see, expanding your business beyond Etsy has its benefits and its downfalls. If you are simply wanting to add more products to your offerings beyond the category you are currently selling in, the answer may be to not sell outside of Etsy but rather to open a second Etsy shop. You can have multiple Etsy shops, you just need to sign up for different accounts, which means you need to use different email addresses. You can easily get a second email address through Google using their Gmail service.

To open a second Etsy account and therefore a new Etsy shop, simply repeat the process we covered earlier in this book. Again, you will need a different email address from your first account.

Etsy allows sellers to have multiple shops, but there are some restrictions. For example, you can't have two shops selling the same items, and you can't use a second shop to get around Etsy's rules or policies. You also have to list all of your shops in the public profile section of each of your Etsy accounts. Even though you need a different email to start a second Etsy shop, you can use the same banking information as you do for your first shop. You will also use the sale taxpayer ID information.

Note that sometimes new shops are automatically flagged by Etsy's automation "bot" system, which is set up to thwart bogus accounts. If this happens to you, you will receive an email. But don't panic. You will simply need to contact Etsy to let them know that you indeed started a second Etsy account as you are opening a second shop. They will ask you to confirm your information. It may take a few days, but Etsy will eventually approve your new account for your new shop.

When would opening a second Etsy shop make sense? It is only beneficial if the products you are selling are in completely different categories. Let's say your first shop is for your handmade jewelry. But you also knit newborn baby blankets. These two products are in different categories and target different customers. In this example, opening a second shop for baby blankets makes sense.

However, let's say that you sell bath bombs but have also started making shower gels, soaps, and body lotions. These products are all in the same bath-and-body category, so keeping them all in one store not only makes sense. Having these products in one shop can also lead to additional sales as they naturally go with one another, meaning customers are more likely to add on to their orders.

Amazon Handmade: *Amazon Handmade* is a section on the Amazon website that features handcrafted items from artisans around the world. It was launched in 2015 as a competitor to Etsy and offers a similar platform for artists and craftspeople to sell their handmade products online.

To sell on *Amazon Handmade*, products must be made entirely by hand, or be altered by hand in a meaningful way. This means that products created with the use of automated equipment or mass-produced products that are later customized by hand are not eligible. Homemade food and beverage items such as baked goods and candy, which can be sold on eBay, are not eligible to be sold on Amazon.

To sell on *Amazon Handmade*, you must apply to be a seller. Unlike other platforms where you can open an account and start selling right away, you need to be approved by Amazon to sell through the program. The application process includes providing detailed information about your products and your crafting process, as well as submitting photos of your products and your workspace. Amazon is very selective about who they approve to sell on their handmade platform.

If you do pass their approval process, note that your handmade items will appear on Amazon's website alongside other products, which gives you the potential to reach a much wider audience than any other platform. Unlike Etsy where you have massive competition from other shops who likely sell similar products as you, there aren't as many sellers in Amazon's *Handmade* program, so in that respect, there is less competition.

Like all platforms, Amazon charges fees for selling on *Handmade*. Amazon charges a referral fee on each item sold, which is a percentage of the item's sale price. There is also a monthly subscription fee for professional selling accounts. And then there are the payment processing fees. In addition, there are advertising opportunities available that you can pay for. But with the higher fees come more exposure.

Facebook Marketplace: If you've been selling your crafts locally, you may have already experimented with selling through Facebook Marketplace. Facebook users can post items for sale for local pick up or shipping. There are no fees involved for local pick-up items, but if you offer to ship, there may be fees. These vary, depending on the promotions the platform runs for sellers. Facebook handles the payment and shipping labels for orders, which is a benefit.

To check for competition, do a search on Facebook Marketplace for the items you sell. If others are selling the same products, check their location. If they offer only local pickup but you're willing to ship orders, you'll have an advantage. And if you have already been shipping orders through Etsy, then managing Facebook shipping will be easy.

If you offer local pickup, you'll need to implement a payment system for customers. Most sellers use PayPal, Venmo, or CashApp, but some also accept cash or checks. If you offer to ship, Facebook provides payment processing and shipping labels. They sometimes even offer promotions where they pay for the shipping, although this is not something you can count on.

The biggest problem with selling items on Facebook Marketplace is meeting people in person. Facebook is notorious for buyers reaching out to sellers, expressing interest in a product, and then disappearing before completing the sale. Or they may consistently reschedule pick-up times and locations. However, if you are patient and available for arranging pickup times, Facebook Marketplace can be a great way to expand your business, especially if you implement an immediate payment system so that people can't flake on you.

eBay: eBay is the third largest online marketplace in America, behind Amazon and Walmart. And while most people think of eBay as the place to score deals on secondhand goods, eBay can be a good place to sell crafts.

Firstly, it's a global marketplace with millions of buyers, which means you have the potential to reach a larger audience than you can on Etsy. Secondly, eBay has a wide range of categories, including a dedicated "Handmade" category, so you can easily list your crafts and have them seen by people who are specifically looking for crafted items.

Additionally, eBay offers various tools and resources to help sellers optimize their listings, manage their inventory, and track their sales. eBay's listing process is similar to Etsy's, so if you are comfortable using

Etsy, using eBay won't be too much of a stretch to learn. eBay also handles payment processing, sales tax collection and remittance, and shipping labels, just like Etsy does, meaning you don't have to worry about coordinating those tasks. Just as Etsy handles all of the backend operations, so does eBay.

All that being said, whether or not eBay is a good place to sell crafts depends on a few factors. For one, competition can be high, especially in popular categories like jewelry and home decor. It can also be difficult to stand out among the millions of listings on the platform, so, just like Etsy, it's important to have high-quality photos and detailed descriptions that accurately showcase your crafts. While Etsy has two shop subscriptions, one free and one for $10, eBay offers several different store subscriptions that come with numerous benefits. You can also customize your eBay store, although the options are limited.

And just like all of the other online selling sites, eBay has its own set of fees. Store subscription fees, listing fees, and final value fees, not to mention optional marketing fees, all eat into your profits. However, eBay is the most similar platform to Etsy in terms of listing and shipping, making it easy to expand there if you already have an established Etsy shop.

Poshmark: Poshmark is a platform primarily focused on fashion, accessories, and beauty items. While you may be able to sell some crafts on Poshmark, it's not necessarily the best platform for selling handmade items. Poshmark is designed for selling new or gently used clothing, so there isn't a specific category for handmade crafts.

That being said, some sellers have had success selling products such as handmade clothes, especially for children. Jewelry, home décor, and bath products all have categories on Poshmark.

The nice thing about selling on Poshmark is that there are no fees to list items for sale there. You only pay fees when an item sells. Poshmark handles payment processing, tax collection, and shipping labels, depositing the remaining profits into your account. So, like Etsy, Amazon, and eBay, the backend work is handled for you, allowing you to focus on creating products, listing them, and shipping orders.

Poshmark sellers are very active on social media, especially Instagram and YouTube. By utilizing those two platforms, you can connect with other Poshmark sellers and grow your following on the site. And since there aren't as many crafters on Poshmark as are on Etsy, there is less competition there.

Mercari: Mercari is an e-commerce platform that is similar to eBay in that it allows people to sell a wide variety of items, both new and secondhand. While it doesn't have as large a user base as eBay, it is very user-friendly, making it easy to list and ship items through the site. Mercari also handles all payments, sales tax, and shipping processing, just as Etsy, eBay, and Poshmark do.

Sellers can list items for sale on Mercari for free, only paying fees when a product sells. The fee is lower than those of eBay and Poshmark; however, the customer base is much smaller than those platforms. Additionally, since customers mainly shop on Mercari for rock-bottom deals, it may not be the best place to sell higher-priced items such as handmade products. However, if you sell lower-priced goods or want to liquidate excess inventory or supplies, not having to pay any listing fees is an advantage as your listings remain on the site for free until they sell.

WhatNot: WhatNot is a relatively new e-commerce platform that initially started as a live auction site for sellers of Funko collectibles, but has since expanded to include numerous categories, including crafts under the **Arts & Handmade** category. Subcategories include

Quilting & Sewing, Knitting & Crochet, Jewelry Making Supplies, Art & Prints, Other Artisan & Handmade Goods, and **Other Art & Craft Supplies**. There is also a **Food & Drink** category for those who sell baked goods and candy.

Sellers can use WhatNot in two ways: live-streaming auctions and buy-it-now listings. Live streaming allows sellers to go live on the app to showcase their products in real-time, enabling buyers to ask questions and interact with the seller, creating a more personalized shopping experience. While most sellers run auctions, you can also sell items at a fixed price during a live sale. Additionally, sellers can list items in the **WhatNot Marketplace** section, which gives sellers a sort of storefront to list products outside of a live sale.

WhatNot's dedicated category for handmade crafts and artisan goods can be an advantage for sellers looking to reach a specific audience. The live-streaming feature provides a unique opportunity for sellers to showcase their handmade items and engage with potential buyers. However, as a newer platform, the user base may not be as large as other online marketplaces, so it's important to research the platform and its audience before deciding whether to sell on WhatNot or another platform. Start with lower-priced items or excess supplies to learn the platform before offering your fixed-price items.

WhatNot's fees are relatively low, and, as with the other sites we've discussed, the platform handles payment processing, tax collection, and shipping labels. The listing process is simple, straightforward, and user-friendly. You only need to enter a short title and shipping weight to list an item at auction or fixed price. You don't even need to upload a photo for an auction, although it is advisable to do so.

Despite being a relatively new platform, WhatNot is growing every day. WhatNot is often described as a social media platform with a selling element. Successful WhatNot sellers not only bring good merchandise to their sales but also run entertaining shows, often implementing giveaways and games to engage buyers. However, most crafters cannot risk running their items at auction, which puts them at a disadvantage as most customers come to WhatNot for the auctions first, and the fixed-price items are an additional offering.

A good tactic for selling crafts on WhatNot is to have live sales where you sell excess crafting supplies at auction while you list your finished products in the **Buy Now** section. This approach allows you to showcase your products live and possibly offer one as a giveaway to entice viewers to buy them outright while you sell off supplies you aren't using.

Shopify: For sellers who want to start their own website, Shopify is often the go-to choice. It provides a powerful and customizable platform for selling your own products, including handmade crafts. With a user-friendly interface and a variety of features to showcase your brand, Shopify can be an effective way to reach a wider audience and grow your business without many limitations.

One of the main advantages of Shopify is its scalability. It's able to handle stores of all sizes, making it a good choice for small businesses and larger enterprises alike. With a range of pricing plans to choose from, Shopify can also be customized to fit a variety of needs and budgets.

However, unlike other selling platforms such as Etsy, Amazon, eBay, Poshmark, Mercari, WhatNot, and Facebook Marketplace, sellers on Shopify need to implement their own payment processing, sales tax collection, and shipping services. This means that sellers need to figure out how to accept payments, collect and remit sales tax for the American states or countries that require it, and incorporate a way to print shipping labels on their own. For many small businesses, especially sole proprietors, this can be overwhelming and time-consuming.

To address the needs of sellers, Shopify offers a variety of payment processing options, including Shopify Payments, PayPal, and other third-party payment gateways. Additionally, Shopify offers tools and integrations for sales tax calculation and shipping label printing to help streamline the process. However, these services vary depending on your location and still require you to set up these third-party providers yourself to integrate them into Shopify.

While having your own dedicated website does give you complete control over your brand, I know many sellers who opened a Shopify store only to eventually close it and return to Etsy and other platforms that handle the back-end processes of running an e-commerce business. The collection and remittance of the sales tax alone is enough for many sellers, including myself, to stick with the established websites that handle those services.

Expand Locally: If expanding to other online selling platforms seems like too much, you can still grow your craft business locally by seeking out additional vendor shows in your area, not just craft fairs but also farmers markets and other area events. Look for craft shows in the surrounding towns; you may have exhausted all of the options in your city, but there may be more beyond your county.

Another idea is to approach local stores and boutiques to sell your products in. Consider researching stores in your area that align with your brand and aesthetic and reaching out to the owners or managers with a professional pitch and samples of your products. The shop owner will likely take a cut of your profits, and some may also charge a flat fee. But they will handle payment processing and sales tax remittance. Plus, you won't have to list or ship products or deal with customer service issues.

Some antique malls allow crafters to have booths to sell their items. And in some areas, there are craft-specific malls where only makers have booths. Finally, don't underestimate the power of networking and word-of-mouth marketing. Consider attending local business events and networking groups to connect with other entrepreneurs and potential customers. Encourage satisfied customers to leave reviews and share your products on social media and consider offering referral incentives to help spread the word about your handmade crafts.

By thinking outside of the box, you may find more opportunities to sell your crafts locally than you realized existed!

CONCLUSION

Congratulations on finishing the *Beginner's Guide To Selling Crafts On Etsy*! By now, you should have a solid understanding of the ins and outs of running an Etsy shop and the steps involved in starting or expanding a successful handmade crafts business.

While the information I've provided may be overwhelming at first, I encourage you to take one step at a time. Open an Etsy account and work on creating a storefront using the free *Etsy Standard* plan. Practice creating listings by keeping them in drafts before you have the confidence to make them live. Play around with the shop design features. If a listing goes live but you have second thoughts, you can end it or just change the available quantity to zero. You can also edit your listings at any time. No Etsy listings are permanent. You have total control of what to list and when to make listings live.

As we've covered, Etsy is the best platform for selling handmade crafts online. With its user-friendly interface and a large and engaged customer base, Etsy provides a unique opportunity for creative entrepreneurs to showcase their handmade goods and connect with customers from around the world. And if you haven't yet begun to develop your handmade goods, hopefully, the ideas covered earlier in this book have you thinking about products to create.

While there is no one-size-fits-all approach to selling crafts on Etsy, I hope that the information and tips provided in this guide have given you a solid foundation for building and growing your handmade crafts business. Remember, building a successful Etsy business takes time, effort, and patience, but with hard work and dedication, you can turn your passion for crafting into a thriving online business.

I wish you the best of luck on your Etsy journey, and hope that you'll continue to explore and experiment with new strategies for growing and expanding your business in the years to come!

ABOUT THE AUTHOR

Ann Eckhart is a writer, entrepreneur, and online content creator based in Iowa. She has authored numerous books about home-based e-commerce businesses on topics including reselling, self-publishing, print-on-demand, and social media. You can find all her titles at www.AnnEckhart.com[1].

You can follow Ann Eckhart on the following social media platforms:

Facebook @anneckhart

Instagram @ann_marie_eckhart

YouTube @anneckhart

---

1. http://www.AnnEckhart.com

Don't miss out!

Visit the website below and you can sign up to receive emails whenever Ann Eckhart publishes a new book. There's no charge and no obligation.

https://books2read.com/r/B-A-UQFB-EPBTC

BOOKS 2 READ

Connecting independent readers to independent writers.

Also by Ann Eckhart

101 Items To Sell On Ebay
101 Items To Sell On Ebay
101 More Items To Sell On Ebay

2022 Home Based Business Books
Beginner's Guide To Amazon KDP 2022 Edition: How To Create &
Sell Books Using Kindle Direct Publishing
Beginner's Guide To Selling On Ebay 2022 Edition: How To Start &
Grow a Successful Online Reselling Business from Home
Beginner's Guide To YouTube 2022 Edition: How To Start & Grow a
Successful & Profitable YouTube Channel

2023 Home Based Business Books
Beginner's Guide To Selling On Ebay: 2023 Edition

Standalone
2020 Ebay Sourcing Guide
Ebay Seller Secrets

How to Start a YouTube Channel for Fun & Profit
Beginner's Guide To Amazon KDP: 2023 Edition
Beginner's Guide To Starting An Etsy Print-On-Demand Shop
Beginner's Guide To Starting An Etsy Sticker Shop
Beginner's Guide To WhatNot: How To Buy & Sell On The Live Auction Reselling App
Reseller Liquidation Database: The Top 35 Liquidation & Wholesale Companies for Online Sellers
2000+ Printable Products To Sell On Etsy
Beginner's Guide To Selling Digital Products On Etsy
Beginner's Guide To Amazon KDP 2024 Edition
Beginner's Guide To Selling Antiques On Etsy
Beginner's Guide To Selling Crafts On Etsy
Beginner's Guide To Selling On eBay 2024 Edition
Beginner's Guide To Starting a YouTube Channel 2024-2025 Edition

Watch for more at www.SeeAnnSave.com.